THE LITTLE
FRENCH
DICTIONARY
OF
WORD
FAMILIES

Learn more than 2500 words

DYLANE MOREAU

PREFACE

The **Little French Dictionary of Word Families** will help you to develop your vocabulary in no time. The principle is simple, learn more vocabulary from the same word families. From beginners to advanced, everyone can benefit from this little dictionary.

Let see an example in English :

A tooth / Teeth

Why would you stop there when you can learn :

1. A toothpaste

2. A toothbrush

3. A toothache

4. A toothpick

5. The wisdom teeth

6. The tooth fairy

7. Tooth decay

8. ....

Do you see how you can speed up your vocabulary learning in one sitting?

The same principle applies in French. Why would you learn word by word when you can learn **up to 11 words together**?

In this book, you will start with 700 French words, and end up knowing more than 2500 words! Almost four times the knowledge without the difficulty. This little dictionary gets straight to the point, everything has been kept simple, with every word translated in English.

ONLY 6 TYPES OF WORDS

nm | Nom masculin

nf | Nom féminin

v | Verbe

Adj | Adjectif

Adv | Adverbe

Prép | Préposition

A FEW THINGS TO KEEP IN MIND

- **NOUNS** - Nouns in French have genders, they are either "masculin" such as "***un garde***" or "féminin" such as "***une dent***". You can find the gender by the article in front of the noun.

Masculine nouns : Un (a) - Le (the)

Feminine nouns : Une (a) - La (the)

When the noun starts with a vowel, the article might be "L'", in this case you can find the indication of the gender by the noun: **(nm)** for "masculin" - **(nf)** for "féminin"

It's important to learn the gender at the same time of the word itself. If you don't learn the gender right away, you will have to learn it later and it will make your learning process longer.

- **ADJECTIVES** - Adjectives in French also change whether the gender of the noun that they describe is masculine or feminine.

For example : "***Sérieux - Sérieuse***"

The masculine version of the adjective is always first, followed by the feminine version.

Please note that this doesn't apply when the adjective ends with "e", it stays the same no matter the gender.

For example : "***Magnifique***"

Translation between 2 languages doesn't always work word for word. The sentences can seem different, but they have the same meaning. Sentence structure can be tricky, keep an open mind.

With all this information, you are ready to start!

TABLE OF CONTENTS

Aa.

ABANDON
1. Un abandon nm | An abandonment
2. Abandonner v | To abandon / To give up
— *Il a **abandonné** ses études l'année dernière* • He abandoned his studies last year

ABORDER
1. Aborder v | To approach / To address
2. Abordable Adj | Approachable / Affordable
— *Il faut **aborder** le problème* • The issue must be addressed

ABRI
1. Un abri nm | A shelter
2. Abriter v | To shelter
3. Un sans-abri nm | A homeless person
— *Le **sans-abri** cherche **un abri** pour la nuit* • The homeless person looks for a shelter for the night

ABSENT
1. Absent - Absente Adj | Absent
2. Une absence nf | An absence
3. S'absenter v | To be absent
— *Cet élève est **absent** aujourd'hui* • This student is absent today

ABSOLU
1. Absolu - Absolue Adj | Absolute
2. Absolument Adv | Absolutely
— *Nous sommes **absolument** enchantés de cette nouvelle* • We are absolutely thrilled with this news

ACCÉLÉRER
1. Accélérer v | To accelerate / To speed up
2. Un accélérateur nm | An accelerator
3. Une accélération nf | An acceleration

— *Il faut* **accélérer** *pour finir le projet* • We have to speed up to finish the project

ACCENT

1. Un accent nm | An accent
2. Accentuer v | To accentuate
3. Une accentuation nf | An accentuation

— *Il y a beaucoup d'***accents** *dans la langue française* • There are a lot of accents in French

ACCEPTER

1. Accepter v | To accept
2. Acceptable Adj | Acceptable
3. Une acceptation nf | Acceptance

— *Le magasin n'***accepte** *pas les cartes de crédit* • The shop doesn't accept credit cards

ACCÈS

1. Accéder v | To access
2. Un accès nm | An access
3. Accessible Adj | Accessible

— *Le musée est* **accessible** *aux personnes à mobilité réduite* • The museum is accessible to persons with reduced mobility

ACCIDENT

1. Un accident nm | An accident
2. Accidentel - Accidentelle Ajd | Accidental / Unintentional

— *Le rapport dit que l'incident était* **accidentel** • The rapport says that the incident was accidental

ACCOMPAGNER

1. Accompagner v | To accompany
2. Un accompagnement nm | A support

— *Les personnes âgées ont besoin d'un* **accompagnement** *quotidien* • Elderly need daily support

ACCOMPLIR

1. Accomplir v | To accomplish / To perform
2. Accompli - Accomplie Adj | Well-rounded
3. Un accomplissement nm | An achievement
— **Accomplir** cette tâche était très difficile • To perform this task was very hard

ACCORDER

1. Accorder v | To grant
2. Un accord nm | An agreement
3. Être d'accord | To agree
— *Je **suis d'accord** avec toi !* • I agree with you!

ACCRO

1. Accrocher v | To hang / To hook
2. Une accroche nf | A hook
3. Un accrochage nm | A car accident
4. Un accro nm | A junkie
5. Une accro nf | A junkie
6. Accro Adj | Addicted
— *Mon frère est **accro** à la caféine* • My brother is addicted to caffeine

ACCUSER

1. Accuser v | To accuse
2. Un accusé nm | Accused
3. Une accusée nf | Accused
4. Une accusation nf | An accusation
— *L'**accusé** a été reconnu coupable* • The accused was found guilty

ACHETER

1. Acheter v | To purchase / To buy
2. Un achat nm | A purchase
3. Un acheteur nm | A purchaser / A buyer
4. Une acheteuse nf | A purchaser / A buyer

3

— *L'**acheteur** potentiel fait une offre pour la maison* • The potential buyer makes an offer for the house

ACHEVER

1. Achever nm | To complete
2. Un achèvement nm | A completion

— *Son neveu a **achevé** sa formation avec succès* • His nephew completed his training with success

ACTION

1. Une action nf | An action
2. Actionner v | To activate
3. Une réaction nf | A reaction

— *Tu aurais dû voir sa **réaction*** • You should have seen his reaction

ACTIVER

1. Activer v | To activate
2. Activement Adv | Actively
3. Actif - Active Adj | Active
4. Un activiste nm | An activist
5. Une activiste nf | An activist
6. Une activité nf | An activity
7. Une activation nf | An activation

— *Il cherche du travail **activement*** • He is actively looking for a job

ADAPTER

1. Adapter v | To adapt
2. Une adaptation nf | An adaptation
3. Un adaptateur nm | An adapter
4. Adaptable Adj | Adaptable

— *L'**adaptateur** est cassé* • The adapter is broken

ADDITION

1. Additionner v | To add
2. Une addition nf | An addition / A bill

3. Additionnel - Additionnelle Adj | Additional

— *Après le repas, le serveur a apporté l'**addition*** • After the meal, the server brought the bill.

ADMINISTRER

1. Administrer v | To administer
2. Une administration nf | An administration
3. Un administrateur nm | An administrator
4. Une administratrice nf | An administrator
5. Administratif - Administrative Adj | Administrative

— *L'**administration** est toujours très lente en décembre* • The administration is always slow in December

ADMIRER

1. Admirer v | To admire
2. Une admiration nf | An admiration
3. Un admirateur nm | An admirer
4. Une admiratrice nf | An admirer
5. Admirable Adj | Admirable

— *Vous pouvez **admirer** les oiseaux du balcon* • You can admire the birds from the balcony

ADOLESCENT

1. Un adolescent nm | A teenager
2. Une adolescente nf | A teenager
3. L'adolescence nf | Adolescence

— *L'**adolescence** est une période difficile pour les parents* • Adolescence is a difficult period for parents

ADOPTER

1. Adopter v | To adopt
2. Une adoption nf | An adoption
3. Adoptable Adj | Adoptable
4. Adoptif-Adoptive Adj | Adoptive

— Une **adoption** *est une bonne alternative* • Adoption is a good alternative

ADORER

1. Adorer v | To adore
2. Adorable Adj | Adorable
3. Une adoration nf | An adoration

  — *Ce chiot est* **adorable** *!* • This puppy is adorable!

ADRESSER

1. Adresser v | To address
2. Une adresse nf | An address

  — *Cette* **adresse** *est erronée* • This address is wrong

ADROIT

1. Adroit - Adroite Adj | Clever
2. Adroitement Adv | Cleverly
3. Maladroit - Maladroite Adj | Awkward
4. Maladroitement Adv | Awkwardly

  — *Il est tellement* **maladroit**, *il casse toujours tout !* • He is so awkward, he always breaks everything!

AFFECTER

1. Affecter v | To affect
2. L'affection nf | An affection
3. Affectueux - Affectueuse Adj | Affectionate

  — *Contrairement à ce que l'on croyait, le chat est très* **affectueux** *envers notre nouveau chien* • Contrary to what we thought, the cat is very affectionate towards our new dog

AFFICHER

1. Afficher v | To display
2. Une affiche nf | A poster
3. Un affichage nm | A display

— *Est-ce que tu as vu **l'affiche** pour le marché de Noël ?* • Have you seen the poster for the Christmas Market?

AFFREUX

1. Affreux - Affreuse Adj | Terrible / Ugly
2. Affreusement Adv | Terribly

— *Quel **affreux** pullover !* • What an ugly sweater!

ÂGE

1. Un âge nm | An age
2. Un anti-âge nm | An anti-age
3. Le troisième âge nm | Old age

— *Il y a un **âge** pour tout* • There is an age for everything

AGRESSER

1. Agresser v | To attack
2. Agressif - Agressive Adj | Aggressive
3. Agressivement Adv | Aggressively
4. L'agressivité nf | Aggression
5. Une agression nf | An aggression
6. Un agresseur nm | An aggressor

— *L'**agresseur** a été arrêté deux jours après l'**agression*** • The aggressor was arrested two days after the aggression

AGRICOLE

1. Agricole Adj | Agricultural
2. Un agriculteur nm | A farmer
3. Une agricultrice nf | A farmer
4. L'agriculture nf | Agriculture

— *Le secteur **agricole** du pays se porte bien* • The agriculture sector of the country is thriving

AIMABLE

1. Aimable Adj | Kind
2. Aimablement Adv | Kindly

3. L'amabilité nf | The kindness
— *Cette serveuse n'est pas très* **aimable** • This waitress is not very kind

AJUSTER
1. Ajuster v | To adjust
2. Un ajustement nm | An adjustment
3. Ajustable Adv | Adjustable
— *Ce pantalon de grossesse est* **ajustable** • These maternity pants are adjustable

ALIMENT
1. Un aliment nm | Food
2. Une alimentation nf | An alimentation
3. Alimentaire Adj | Dietary
4. Alimenter v | To feed
5. Sous-alimenter v | To undernourish
6. Suralimenter v | To overfeed
— *Une* **alimentation** *équilibrée contient des fruits et des légumes* • A healthy diet contains fruits and vegetables

ALLERGIE
1. Une allergie nf | An allergy
2. Allergique Adj | Allergic
3. Un allergène nm | Allergen
— *Marie est* **allergique** *aux cacahuètes* • Marie is allergic to peanuts

ALLIER
1. Allier v | To ally
2. Une alliance nf | An alliance
3. Une alliance nf | A wedding ring
4. Un allié nm | An ally
5. Une alliée nf | An ally
— *Elle est probablement mariée car elle porte une* **alliance** • She is probably married because she wears a wedding ring

8

ALTERNER

1. Alterner v | To alternate
2. Une alternative nf | An alternative
3. Alternatif - Alternative Adj | Alternative
4. Une alternance nf | An alternation

— *Le soja est une bonne **alternative** à la viande* • Soy is a good alternative to meat

AMÉLIORER

1. Améliorer v | To improve
2. Une amélioration nf | An improvement

— *Ce projet pourrait être **amélioré** par mon équipe* • This project could be improved by my team

AMI

1. Un ami nm | A friend
2. Une amie nf | A friend
3. Une amitié nf | A friendship
4. Amical Adj | Friendly
5. Amicalement Adv | Friendly
6. Un petit-ami nm | A boyfriend
7. Une petite-amie nf | A girlfriend
8. Un meilleur ami nm | A best friend
9. Une meilleure amie nf | A best friend

— *Mon **meilleur ami** habite en Australie* • My best friend lives in Australia

AMOUR

1. L'amour nm | Love
2. Amoureux - Amoureuse Adj | In love
3. Un amoureux nm | A lover
4. Une amoureuse nf | A lover

— *Il est **amoureux** de sa voisine* • He is in love with his neighbor

AMUSER

1. Amuser v | To amuse
2. Amusant - Amusante Adj | Funny / Amusing
3. Un amusement nm | An amusement

—— *Cette histoire ne **m'amuse** pas beaucoup !* • This story doesn't amuse me!

AN

1. Un an nm | A year
2. Une année nf | A year
3. Annuel - Annuelle Adj | Annual
4. Annuellement Adv | Annually
5. Un anniversaire nm | An anniversary / A birthday

—— *Chaque **année**, nous organisons une fête pour son anniversaire* • Every year we organize a party for his birthday

ANALYSER

1. Analyser v | To analyse
2. Une analyse nf | An analyse
3. Un analyste nm | An analyst
4. Une analyste nf | An analyst

—— *Une **analyse** a démontré que la société ne fait pas de bénéfices* • An analyse demonstrated that the company doesn't have any profits

ANIMAL

1. Un animal nm | An animal
2. Animalier - Animalière Adj | Animal
3. Un animal domestique nm | A pet
4. Un animal sauvage nm | A wild animal

—— *Un cochon peut être **un animal domestique*** • A pig can be a pet

ANNONCER

1. Annoncer v | To announce
2. Une annonce nf | An ad
3. Un annonceur nm | An advertiser

4. Une annonceuse nf | An advertiser

— *Il y a trop d'**annonces** à la télévision* • There are too many
ads on television

ANTICIPER

1. Anticiper v | To anticipate
2. Une anticipation nf | An anticipation

— *Nous avions **anticipé** cette dépense* • We anticipated this expense

ANXIEUX

1. Anxieux - Anxieuse Adj | Anxious
2. Anxieusement Adv | Anxiously
3. L'Anxiété nf | Anxiety
4. Un anxiolytique nm | Anxiolytic

— *Mes parents sont **anxieux** de prendre l'avion* • My parents are
anxious to fly

APPARAÎTRE

1. Apparaître v | To appear
2. Une apparition nf | An appearance

— *Il **apparait** qu'il ne connait rien à l'informatique* • It appears
that he doesn't know anything about computer science

APPARTENIR

1. Appartenir v | To belong
2. Une appartenance nf | A belonging
3. Appartenant Adv | Belonging

— *Ce manteau **appartient** à mon frère* • This coat belongs to
my brother

APPEL

1. Un appel nm | A call
2. Une appellation nf | A designation
3. Appeler v | To call
4. S'appeler v | To be called

— *La banque doit m'**appeler** demain matin* • The bank should call me tomorrow morning

APPLAUDIR
1. Applaudir v | To applaud
2. Un applaudissement nm | An applause

— *Le show s'est clôturé par des **applaudissements*** • The show ended with a round of applause

APPLIQUER
1. Appliquer v | To apply
2. Une application nf | An application
3. Applicable Adj | Applicable

— *Il pense que les règles ne s'**appliquent** qu'aux autres* • He thinks rules only apply to others

APPORT
1. Un apport nm | A contribution
2. Apporter v | To bring

— *Nous **apporterons** une tarte à la fraise* •We will bring a strawberry pie

APPRÉCIER
1. Apprécier v | To appreciate
2. Une appréciation nf | An appreciation
3. Appréciable Adj | Appreciable

— *Ta carte a été très **appréciée*** • Your card was very appreciated

APPRENDRE
1. Apprendre v | To learn
2. Appris - Apprise Adj | Learned
3. Un apprenti nm | An apprentice
4. Une apprentie nf | An apprentice
5. Un apprentissage nm | An apprenticeship

— **Appprendre** *une nouvelle langue est enrichissant* • Learning a new language is rewarding

APPROCHER
1. Approcher v | To approach
2. Une approche nf | An approach
— *Je me suis **approchée** lentement* • I approached slowly

APPROXIMATIF
1. Approximatif - Approximative Adj | Approximate
2. Approximativement Adv | Approximately
3. Une approximation nf | An approximation
— *Les mesures sont **approximatives*** • Measurements are approximate

APRÈS
1. Après Adv | After
2. Un après rasage nm | An aftershave
3. Un après shampoing nm | A conditioner
4. Un après-midi nm | An afternoon
5. Après-demain Adv | The day after tomorrow
6. Un après-ski nm | An après-ski
7. Un après-soleil nm | An after-sun lotion
8. Un service après-vente nm | A customer service
— *Il faut toujours mettre de **l'après-soleil** après une journée à la plage* • You should always apply after-sun lotion after a day at the beach

ARCHITECTURE
1. L'architecture nf | The architecture
2. Un architecte nm | An architect
3. Une architecte nf | An architect
4. Architectural Adj | Architectural
— *Cet **architecte** a beaucoup de talent* • This architect has a lot of talent

ARME

1. Une arme nf | A weapon
2. L'armée nf | The army
3. Un armurier nm | A gunsmith
4. Une armurerie nf | An armoury
5. Armer v | To arm

— *Le policier est **armé** de son pistolet* • The police officer is armed with his gun

ARRANGER

1. Arranger v | To arrange
2. Un arrangement nm | An arrangement
3. Arrangeant - Arrangeante Adj | Accommodating

— *Elle **arrange** la nourriture dans le garde-manger* • She arranges the food in the pantry

ARRÊT

1. Un arrêt nm | A stop
2. Arrêter v | To stop

— *Le bus s'**arrête** à chaque **arrêt*** • The bus stops at every stop

ARRIVER

1. Arriver v | To arrive
2. Un arrivage nm | An arrival
3. Une arrivée nf | An arrival

— *Le train est **arrivé** avec une heure de retard* • The train arrived an hour late

ARROGANCE

1. L'arrogance nf | Arrogance
2. Arrogant - Arrogante Adj | Arrogant

— *L'**arrogance** ne te mènera nulle part* • Arrogance won't bring you anywhere

ARROSER

1. Arroser v | To water
2. L'arrosage nm | The watering
3. Un arrosoir nm | A watering can
4. Un tuyau d'arrosage nm | A hose

— *Il y a un trou dans le **tuyau d'arrosage*** • There is a hole in the hose

ART

1. L'art nm | The art
2. Un artiste nm | An artist
3. Une artiste nf | An artist
4. Artistique Adj | Artistic
5. Artistiquement Adv | Artistically
6. Un artisan nm | An artisan
7. Artisanal - Artisanale Adj | Handmade
8. L'artisanat nm | The craft

— *Une sculpture **artisanale** peut se vendre plusieurs milliers d'euros*
• A handmade sculpture can be sold for few thousands of euros

ASPIRER

1. Aspirer v | To vacuum
2. Un aspirateur nm | A vacuum
3. Une aspiration nf | A suction

— *L'**aspirateur** est bouché, il n'**aspire** plus* • The vacuum is blocked, it doesn't vacuum anymore

ASSISTER

1. Assister v | To assist
2. Une assistance nf | An assistance
3. Un assistant nm | An assistant
4. Une assistante nf | An assistant

— *Son **assistant** sera avec lui durant ce voyage d'affaires* • His assistant will be with him during this business trip

ASSOCIER

1. Associer v | To associate
2. Un associé nm | A partner
3. Une associée nf | A partner
4. Une association nf | An association

— *Cette **association** s'occupe des chiens abandonnés* • This association takes care of abandoned dogs

ASSURER

1. Assurer v | To ensure / To insure
2. Une assurance nf | Insurance
3. Un assureur nm | An insurer

— *L'**assurance** du véhicule est expirée* • The vehicle insurance is expired

ATTAQUE

1. Une attaque nf | An attack
2. Un attaquant nm | An attacker
3. Une attaquante nf | An attacker
4. Attaquer v | To attack

— *L'**attaque** s'est produite à 22 heures* • The attack happened at 10pm

ATTENTE

1. Une attente nf | A wait
2. Une salle d'attente nf | A waiting room
3. Attendre v | To wait
4. En attendant Adv | Meanwhile

— *Les patients sont dans la **salle d'attente*** • Patients are in the waiting room

ATTENTION

1. Faire attention | To be careful / To pay attention
2. Une attention nf | An attention
3. Attentionné - Attentionnée Adj | Attentive
4. Une inattention nf | An inattention

— *Tu dois faire **attention** en traversant la route* • You need to pay attention while crossing the road

ATTIRER

1. Attirer v | To attract
2. Une attirance nf | An attraction
3. Attirant - Attirante Adj | Attractive / Tempting

— *Le salaire proposé est très **attirant*** • The proposed salary is really tempting

AUSSI

1. Aussi Adv | Also
2. Aussitôt Adv | As soon as

— *Je suis venu **aussitôt** que j'ai eu la nouvelle* • I came as soon as I got the news

AUTO

1. Une autoroute nf | A highway
2. Un autocar nf | A coach
3. Un autobus nf | A bus
4. Une automobile nf | A car
5. Un autopilote nm | Autopilot

— *L'**autobus** prend l'**autoroute*** • The bus takes the highway

AUTOMNE

1. Un automne nm | An autumn
2. Automnal - Automnale Adj | Autumnal

— *L'**automne** est une saison pleine de couleurs* • Autumn is a season full of colour

AUTORISER

1. Autoriser v | To allow
2. Une autorisation nf | A permit

— *Ma banque **autorise** les retraits à l'étranger* • My bank allows withdrawals abroad

AVANCE

1. Une avance nf | An advance
2. Un avancement nm | An advancement
3. Avancer v | To move forward
4. En avance Adv | In advance / Early

—— *Le juge arrive **en avance** pour revoir ses dossiers* • The judge arrives early to review his files

AVANTAGER

1. Un avantage nm | An advantage
2. Avantageux - Avantageuse Adj | Advantageous

—— *Parler plusieurs langues est un **avantage*** • Speaking several languages is an advantage

AVENTURER

1. Aventurer v | To adventure
2. Une aventure nf | An adventure
3. Un aventurier nm | An adventurer
4. Une aventurière nf | An adventurer
5. Aventureux - Aventureuse Adj | Adventurous

—— *Mon voyage au Mexique était une **aventure** magnifique* • My trip to Mexico was a wonderful adventure

AVERTIR

1. Avertir v | To warn
2. Un avertissement nm | A warning

—— *L'élève reçoit un **avertissement** de son professeur* • The student gets a warning from his professor

AVORTER

1. Avorter v | To abort
2. Un avortement nm | An abortion

—— *Le médecin se charge des **avortements*** • The doctor is in charge of abortions

Bb.

BAIN

1. Un bain nm | A bath
2. Une baignoire nf | A bathtub
3. Une baignade nf | A swim
4. Se baigner v | To bathe
5. Le maillot de bain nm | A swimsuit

— *Rien de tel qu'un **bain** chaud après une journée dehors* • Nothing like a warm bath after a day outside

BALANCE

1. Une balance nf | A scale / A balance
2. Balancer v | To balance / To scale / To rock
3. Une balançoire nf | A swing

— *Il **balance** le berceau pour que le bébé s'endorme* • He rocks the cradle so the baby falls asleep

BALAYER

1. Balayer v | To sweep
2. Un balayeur nm | A sweeper
3. Une balayette nf | A hand brush
4. Un balayage nf | A scan
5. Un balai nm | A broom

— *Le **balai** est dans le placard* • The broom is in the closet

BALLE

1. Une balle nf | A ball
2. Un ballon nm | A ball / A balloon
3. Un ballot nm | A bundle

— *Passe-moi la **balle** !* • Give me the ball!

BANANE

1. Une banane nm | A banana
2. Un bananier nm | A banana tree

— *Le **bananier** est un arbre d'Afrique* • The banana tree is from Africa

BANDE

1. Une bande nf | A band / A strip
2. Un bandage nm | A bandage
3. Bander v | To bandage
4. Un bandeau nm | A headband
5. Une bande dessinée nf | A comic book
6. Une banderole nf | A banner

— *Les joueurs de tennis portent des **bandeaux*** • Tennis players wear headbands

BANQUE

1. Une banque nf | A bank
2. Un banquier nm | A banker
3. Une banquière nf | A banker

— *J'ai ouvert un compte épargne à la **banque*** • I opened a savings account at the bank

BARBE

1. Une barbe nm | A beard
2. Barbu Adj | Bearded
3. Un barbier nm | A barber

— *Devenir **barbier** est populaire de nos jours* • Becoming a barber is popular nowadays

BASE

1. La base nf | The base
2. Basique Adj | Basic
3. Basiquement Adv | Basically

— *Le calcul est la **base** des mathématiques* • Calculus is the base of mathematics

BATAILLE

1. Une bataille nf | A fight / A battle
2. Batailler v | To flight / To battle
3. Se battre v | To fight

22

4. Battre v | To beat

— *Les soldats ont gagné la **bataille*** • The soldiers won the battle

BEAU

1. Beau Adj | Beautiful
2. La beauté nf | The beauty
3. Un salon de beauté nm | A beauty salon
4. Un beau-frère nm | A brother-in-law
5. Un beau-père nm | A stepfather / A father-in-law
6. Un beau-fils nm | A stepson / A son-in-law

— *Je te présente Mark, mon **beau-frère*** • Let me introduce Mark, my brother-in-law

BELLE

1. Belle Adj | Beautiful
2. Une belle-fille nf | A daughter-in-law
3. Une belle-mère nf | A stepmother / A mother-in-law
4. Une belle-sœur nf | A sister-in-law

— *C'est une **belle** victoire pour l'équipe* • It's a beautiful victory for the team

BÉNÉFICE

1. Un bénéfice nm | A profit
2. Bénéficier v | To profit
3. Un bénéficiaire nm | A beneficiary
4. Une bénéficiaire nf | A beneficiary
5. Bénéfique Adj | Beneficial

— *Cette année à l'étranger lui a été très **bénéfique*** • This year abroad was very beneficial to him

BLANC

1. Blanc - Blanche Adj | White
2. Blanchi - Blanchie Adj | White-washed
3. Le blanchisseur nm | The whitener
4. La blancheur nf | The whiteness

5. Blanchir v | To launder

6. Une nuit blanche nf | A sleepless night

— *Je ne pouvais pas dormir, j'ai passé une **nuit blanche*** • I couldn't sleep, I had a sleepless night

BLESSER

1. Blesser v | To injure

2. Une blessure nf | An injury

3. Un blessé nm | An injured person

4. Une blessée nf | An injured person

— *Le patient souffre d'une **blessure** à la jambe* • The patient suffers from a leg injury

BLOC

1. Un bloc nm | A block

2. Un blocage nm | A blockage

3. Bloquer v | To block

— *La police **bloque** la rue après un accident* • The police block the street after an accident

BOIRE

1. Boire v | To drink

2. Une boisson nf | A drink

— *Veux-tu **boire** quelque chose ?* • Would you like something to drink?

BOIS

1. Le bois nm | The woods

2. Du bois nm | Some wood

3. Boisé Adj | Woody

— *Le chien s'est perdu dans les **bois*** • The dog got lost in the woods

BOND

1. Un bond nm | A jump

2. Bondir v | To jump

3. Un rebond nm | A bounce

4. Rebondir v | To bounce
5. Un rebondissement nm | A rebound
— *Le chat **bondit** sur la table* • The cat jumps on the table

BOUCHE

1. La bouche nf | The mouth
2. Une bouchée nf | A bite / A mouthful
3. Un bain de bouche nm | A mouthwash
— *Ne parle pas la **bouche** pleine* • Don't talk with your mouth full

BOUCHER

1. Un boucher nm | A butcher
2. Une boucherie nf | A butcher shop
— *La **boucherie** vende de la viande et de la charcuterie* • The butcher shop sells meat and ham

BOUCLE

1. Une boucle nf | A loop
2. Un bouclage nm | A closure
3. Boucler v | To curl
4. En boucle Adv | Ad infinitum
5. Une boucle d'oreille nf | An earring
— *As-tu vu mes **boucles d'oreilles** en or ?* • Have you seen my gold earrings?

BOUTON

1. Un bouton nm | A button
2. Boutonner v | To button
3. Déboutonner v | To unbutton
4. Une boutonnière nf | A buttonhole
— *J'ai perdu un **bouton** de ma chemise* • I lost a button on my shirt

BRILLER

1. Briller v | To shine

2. Brillant - Brillante Adj | Brilliant

3. Une brillance nf | A brightness

4. Brillamment Adv | Brilliantly

— *Le soleil **brille** dans le ciel* • The sun shines in the sky

BRONZE

1. Le bronze nm | The bronze

2. Bronzer v | To tan

3. Le bronzage nm | The tan

— *Les touristes **bronzent** sur la plage* • Tourists tan on the beach

BROSSE

1. Une brosse nf | A brush

2. Brosser v | To brush

3. Se brosser v | To brush oneself

4. Le brossage nm | The brushing

5. Une brosse à dents nf | A toothbrush

6. Une brosse à cheveux nf | A hairbrush

— *Le matin, il faut **se brosser** les dents et les cheveux* • In the morning, we need to brush our teeth and our hair

BRUIT

1. Un bruit nm | A noise

2. Un bruit de fond nm | A background noise

3. Un bruit sourd nm | A muffled sound

4. Bruyant - Bruyante Adj | Noisy

— *Il y a un **bruit** sourd dans le moteur* • There is a muffled sound in the engine

BRÛLER

1. Brûler v | To burn

2. Une brûlure nf | A burn

3. Brûlant - Brûlante Adj | Burning

4. Un bruleur nm | A burner

— *C'est très chaud, ne te **brûle** pas* • It's really hot, don't burn yourself

BUDGET
1. Un budget nm | A budget
2. Budgétiser v | To budget
3. La budgétisation nf | Budgetisation
— *Il faut **budgétiser** pour économiser* • It's necessary to budget to save

Cc.

CACHER

1. Cacher v | To hide
2. Une cachette nf | A hiding place
3. Un vice caché nm | A hidden defect
4. Cache-cache nm | Hide and seek
   — *Les enfants jouent à **cache-cache*** • Children play hide and seek

CAFÉ

1. Un café nm | A coffee
2. Une cafetière nf | A coffee maker
3. La caféine nf | The caffeine
4. La cafétaria nf | The cafeteria
5. Une pause-café nf | A coffee break
6. Une machine à café nf | A coffee machine
   — *Je prendrai un **café** avec du lait* • I will take a coffee with milk

CALCUL

1. Un calcul nm | A calculation
2. Une calculatrice nf | A calculator
3. Calculer v | To calculate
   — *L'architecte **calcule** les mesures de la maison* • The architect calculates the measurements of the house

CALME

1. Calme Adj | Calm
2. Le calme nm | The calm
3. Calmer v | To calm
4. Un calmant nm | A sedative
   — *La rivière est **calme** le matin* • The river is calm in the morning

CAMION

1. Un camion nm | A truck
2. Une camionnette nf | A van
3. Un camionneur nm | A truck driver
4. Une camionneuse nf | A truck driver

— *L'accident a été causé par un **camion*** •The accident was caused by a truck

CARACTÈRE

1. Un caractère nm | A character
2. Caractériser v | To characterize
3. Une caractéristique nf | A characteristic
4. Caractéristique Adj | Characteristic

— *La maison possède un toit **caractéristique*** • The house has a characteristic roof

CARRÉ

1. Un carré nm | A square
2. Carreler v | To tile
3. Le carrelage nm | The tiling
4. Un carreleur nm | A tiler
5. Un carreau nm | A tile / A window

— *Le **carrelage** de la cuisine est blanc* • The tiling in the kitchen is white

CASSER

1. Casser v | To break
2. Une casse nf | A breakage
3. Une cassure nf | A break
4. Un casse-croute nm | A snack
5. Un casse-tête nm | A puzzle
6. Un casse-cou nm | A daredevil

— *Je n'arrive pas à résoudre ce **casse-tête*** • I can't solve this puzzle

CAUSE

1. Une cause nf | A cause
2. Causer v | To cause

— *La **cause** de l'accident est inconnue* • The cause of the accident is unknown

CÉLÈBRE

1. Célèbre Adj | Famous
2. Célébrer v | To celebrate
3. Une célébration nf | A celebration
4. Une célébrité nf | A celebrity

— *Nous **célébrons** son anniversaire demain* • We celebrate his birthday tomorrow

CENTRE

1. Le centre nm | The center
2. Central - Centrale Adj | Central
3. Centrer v | To center
4. Un centre commercial nm | A mall

— *Elle est au **centre** de l'attention* • She is the center of the attention

CERISE

1. Une cerise nf | A cherry
2. Un cerisier nm | A cherry tree
3. Une tomate cerise nf | A cherry tomato

— *Le Japon est célèbre pour ses **cerisiers*** • Japan is famous for their cherry trees

CERTAIN

1. Certain - Certaine Adj | Certain
2. Certainement Adv | Certainly

— *Il y a **certainement** une autre solution* • There is certainly another solution

CHAGRIN

1. Le chagrin nm | The grief
2. Chagriner v | To grieve

— *Le **chagrin** est une émotion profonde* • Grief is a deep emotion

CHALEUR

1. La chaleur nf | The warmth

2. Chaleureux - Chaleureuse Adj | Warm

— *J'ai reçu un accueil très **chaleureux*** • I got a very warm welcome

CHANCE

1. La chance nf | The luck
2. Chanceux - Chanceuse Adj | Lucky
3. La malchance nf | The badluck
4. Malchanceux - Malchanceuse Adj | Unlucky

— *Pour gagner la loterie il faut avoir de la **chance*** • To win the lottery you need luck

CHANGER

1. Changer v | To change
2. Un changement nm | A change
3. Échanger v | To exchange
4. Un échange nm | An exchange
5. Le taux de change nm | The exchange rate

— *Le **taux de change** est très bas cette semaine* • The exchange rate is very low this week

CHANT

1. Un chant nm | A song
2. Chanter v | To sing
3. Un chanteur nm | A singer
4. Une chanteuse nf | A singer

— *Je **chante** toujours sous la douche* • I always sing in the shower

CHARGE

1. Une charge nf | A charge
2. Charger v | To charge
3. Un chargeur nm | A charger

— *Je dois **charger** mon téléphone* • I need to charge my phone

CHARME

1. Le charme nm | The charm

2. **Charmer** v | To charm
3. **Charmant - Charmante** Adj | Charming
4. **Charmeur - Charmeuse** Adj | Charming
— *La nouvelle voisine est **charmante*** • The new neighbor is charming

CHASSE

1. **La chasse** nf | The hunt
2. **Un chasseur** nm | A hunter
3. **Une chasseuse** nf | A hunter
4. **Chasser** v | To hunt
— *Il va à la **chasse** ce week-end* • He is going hunting this weekend

CHAT

1. **Un chat** nm | A cat
2. **Un chaton** nm | A kitten
3. **Une chatière** nf | A cat flap
— *Le **chat** dort au soleil* • The cat is sleeping in the sun

CHAUD

1. **Chaud - Chaude** Adj | Hot / Warm
2. **Chaudement** Adv | Warmly
3. **Une chaudière** nf | A furnace
4. **Un chaudron** nm | A cauldron
— *La **chaudière** est en panne* • The furnace is broken

CHAUSSURE

1. **Une chaussure** nf | A shoe
2. **Une chaussette** nf | A sock
3. **Un chausson** nm | A slipper
4. **Une chaussée** nf | A road
— *As-tu vu mes **chaussons** ?* • Have you seen my slippers?

CHERCHER

1. **Chercher** v | To search
2. **Une recherche** nf | A research

3. Un chercheur nm | A researcher
4. Une chercheuse nf | A researcher
— *Il faut financer la **recherche** scientifique* • We need to finance scientific research

CHEVEU
1. Un cheveu nm | A hair
2. La chevelure nf | The hair
3. Chevelu - Chevelue Adj | Hairy
4. Une coupe de cheveux nf | A haircut
5. Le cuir chevelu nm | The scalp
— *Que penses-tu de ma nouvelle **coupe de cheveux** ?* • What do you think of my new haircut?

CHIMIE
1. La chimie nf | Chemistry
2. Chimique Adj | Chemical
3. Un chimiste nm | A chemist
4. Une chimiste nf | A chemist
— *La **chimie** n'est pas son point fort* • Chemistry is not his main strength

CHIRURGIE
1. Une chirurgie nf | A surgery
2. Un chirurgien nm | A surgeon
3. Une chirurgienne nf | A surgeon
4. Chirurgical - Chirurgicale Adj | Surgical
— *Le **chirurgien** porte un masque pendant la chirurgie* • The surgeon wears a mask during the surgery

CHUTE
1. Une chute nf | A fall
2. Chuter v | To fall
3. Une chute d'eau nf | A waterfall
— *Les **chutes d'eau** gèlent pendant l'hiver* • Waterfalls freeze during winter

CIGARE

1. Un cigare nm | A cigar
2. Une cigarette nf | A cigarette
3. Un allume-cigare nm | A cigarette lighter

— *Les **cigares** de Cuba sont très populaires* • Cigars from Cuba are really popular

CITRON

1. Un citron nm | A lemon
2. Un citron vert nm | A lime
3. Un citronnier nm | A lemon tree
4. Une citronnade nf | A lemonade

— *J'ai oublié d'acheter un **citron vert*** • I forgot to buy a lime

CLIMAT

1. Le climat nm | The climate
2. Climatiser v | To air-condition
3. La climatisation nf | Air conditioning
4. Le réchauffement climatique nm | Global warming

— *Le **réchauffement climatique** est très inquiétant* • Global warming is very concerning

COIFFER

1. Coiffer v | To style
2. Une coiffure nf | A hairstyle
3. Un coiffeur nm | A hairdresser
4. Une coiffeuse nf | A hairdresser
5. Un salon de coiffure nm | A hair salon

— *J'ai rendez-vous chez le **coiffeur** à 15 heures* • I have an appointment at the hairdresser's at 3pm

COLLE

1. La colle nf | The glue
2. Coller v | To glue
3. Un collage nf | A collage

4. Collant - Collante Adj | Sticky

5. Du papier-collant nm | Some tape

— *J'ai besoin de **papier-collant** pour emballer les cadeaux* • I need tape to wrap the gifts

COLLECTE

1. Une collecte nf | A collection

2. Collecter v | To collect

3. Une collection nf | A collection

4. Un colleteur nm | A collector

5. Une collectrice nf | A collector

— *Sa **collection** de timbres est impressionnante* • His stamps collection is impressive

COMÉDIE

1. Une comédie nf | A comedy

2. Un comédien nm | A comedian

3. Une comédienne nf | A comedian

4. Une comédie musicale nf | A musical comedy

— *Pourquoi ne pas aller voir une **comédie musicale** ?* • Why not go see a musical comedy?

COMMANDE

1. Une commande nf | An order

2. Commander v | To order

3. Un commanditaire nm | A sponsor

4. Une télécommande nf | A remote control

— *Il faut **commander** plus de café* • We need to order more coffee

COMMERCE

1. Un commerce nm | A business

2. Commercial - Commerciale Adj | Commercial

3. Un commercial nm | A sales representative

4. Un commerçant nm | A merchant

5. Une commerçante nf | A merchant

6. La commercialisation nf | The marketing

— *J'aimerais avoir mon propre **commerce*** • I would like to have my own business

COMMUNIQUER

1. Communiquer v | To communicate
2. La communication nf | The communication

— *La **communication** dans le couple est importante* • Communication in a relationship is important

COMPARER

1. Comparer v | To compare
2. Une comparaison nf | A comparison
3. Comparable Adj | Comparable

— *Ne te **compare** pas aux autres* • Don't compare yourself to others

COMPÉTITION

1. Une compétition nf | A competition
2. Compétitif - Compétitive Adj | Competitive
3. Un compétiteur nm | A competitor
4. Une compétitrice nf | A competitor
5. La compétitivité nf | The competitiveness

— *Ce joueur de tennis est très **compétitif*** • This tennis player is very competitive

COMPOSER

1. Composer v | To compose
2. Une composition nf | A composition
3. Un composant nm | A component
4. Un compositeur nm | A composer
5. Une compositrice nf | A composer

— *Mozart était un incroyable **compositeur*** • Mozart was an incredible composer

COMPTER

1. Compter v | To count
2. La comptabilité nf | The accounting
3. Un comptable nm | An accountant
4. Une comptable nf | An accountant
5. Un compteur nm | A counter

— *Envoie les documents au **comptable*** • Send the documents to the accountant

CONDUIRE

1. Conduire v | To drive
2. Un conducteur nm | A driver
3. Une conductrice nf | A driver
4. La conduite nf | The behavior
5. Un permis de conduire nm | A driving license

— *Mon frère a réussi son **permis de conduire*** • My brother got his driving licence

CONFORT

1. Le confort nm | The comfort
2. Confortable Adj | Comfortable

— *Ce fauteuil est très **confortable*** • This armchair is very comfortable

CONGELER

1. Congeler v | To freeze
2. Un congélateur nm | A freezer

— *Le **congélateur** est en panne* • The freezer is broken

CONNAÎTRE

1. Connaître v | To know
2. Une connaissance nf | Knowledge
3. Un connaisseur nm | An expert
4. Une connaisseuse nf | An expert
5. Connaisseur - Connaisseuse Adj | Knowledgeable

— *C'est un **connaisseur** de vins !* • It's an expert in wines!

CONSEIL

1. Un conseil nm | An advice
2. Conseiller v | To advise
3. Un conseiller nm | An advisor

— *Je lui **conseille** d'acheter cette maison* • I advise him to buy this house

CONSOMMER

1. Consommer v | To consume
2. La consommation nf | The consumption
3. Consommable Adj | Consumable
4. Un consommateur nm | A consumer
5. Une consommatrice nf | A consumer

— *La **consommation** de ces dernières années a augmenté significativement* • Consumption has increased significantly these past few years

CONSTRUIRE

1. Construire v | To build
2. La construction nf | The construction
3. Un constructeur nm | A builder

— *La **construction** de la maison prend plus de temps que prévu* • Construction of the house is taking more time than expected

CONSULTER

1. Consulter v | To consult
2. Un consultant nm | A consultant
3. Une consultation nf | A consultation

— *Je **consulterai** mon avocat pour ce contrat* • I will consult my lawyer for this contract

CONTACT

1. Un contact nm | A contact
2. Contacter v | To contact

— *Peux-tu **contacter** le client ce matin ?* • Can you contact the client this morning?

CONTENIR

1. Contenir v | To contain
2. Contenant Adj | Containing
3. Un conteneur nm | A container

—— *Une orange **contient** beaucoup de calcium* • An orange contains a lot of calcium

CONTRAIRE

1. Le contraire nm | The opposite
2. Contrairement Adv | Contrary to
3. Au contraire Adv | On the contrary

—— ***Au contraire**, j'aimerais beaucoup venir !* • On the contrary, I would like to come!

CONTRE

1. Contre Prép | Against / Anti
2. La contrebande nf | The smuggling
3. Une contrepartie nf | A counterparty
4. Un contretemps nm | A setback
5. Une contrefaçon nf | A counterfeit
6. Une contre-indication nf | A contraindication

—— *Je ne pourrai pas venir ce soir, j'ai un **contretemps*** • I will not be able to come tonight, I have a setback

COPAIN

1. Un copain nm | A friend / A boyfriend
2. Une copine nf | A friend / A girlfriend
3. Un petit-copain nm | A boyfriend
4. Une petite-copine nf | A girlfriend

—— *Eric est un de mes **copains** d'enfance* • Eric is one of my childhood friends

COPIE

1. Une copie nf | A copy
2. Copier v | To copy

3. Un copieur nm | A copier

4. Une photocopie nf | A photocopy

5. Un photocopieur nm | A photocopier

— *Peux-tu faire une* **copie** *s'il te plaît ?* • Can you make a copy please?

CORRESPONDRE

1. Correspondre v | To correspond

2. Une correspondance nf | A correspondence

3. Un correspondant nm | A correspondent

4. Une correspondante nf | A correspondent

— *Les résultats devraient* **correspondre** *aux chiffres* • The results should correspond to the numbers

COUCHER

1. Coucher v | To lay down

2. Une couche nf | A layer

3. Une couchette nf | A bunk

4. Un coucher de soleil nm | A sunset

5. Le couchage nm | The berth

6. Une chambre à coucher nf | A bedroom

— *Nous repeignons la* **chambre à coucher** • We are repainting the bedroom

COULEUR

1. Une couleur nf | A colour

2. Colorier v | To colour

3. Un colorant nm | A dye

4. Une coloration nf | A coloration

— *Cette* **couleur** *te va très bien !* • This colour suits you well!

COUPE

1. Une coupe nf | A cut

2. Couper v | To cut

3. Coupant - Coupante Adj | Cutting

— *Je me suis coupée avec le* **couteau** • I cut myself with the knife

COURAGE

1. Le courage nm | The courage
2. Courageux - Courageuse Adj | Courageous
3. Courageusement Adv | Courageously
4. Encourager v | To encourage
5. Les encouragements nm | The encouragements
6. Encourageant - Encourageante Adj | Encouraging

— *Un athlète a besoin d'**encouragements*** • An athlete needs encouragement

COÛT

1. Un coût nm | A cost
2. Coûter v | To cost
3. Coûteux - coûteuse Adj | Costly / Expensive

— *Ce vase est **coûteux**, c'est artisanal* • This vase is expensive, it's handmade

CRÉER

1. Créer v | To create
2. Une création nf | A creation
3. La créativité nf | The creativity
4. Une créature nf | A creature
5. Un créateur nm | A creator
6. Une créatrice nf | A creator

— *Il **crée** de magnifiques tableaux* • He creates incredible paintings

CRÈME

1. La crème nf | The cream
2. Crémeux - Crémeuse Adj | Creamy
3. Le crémier nm | The creamer
4. La crémière nf | The creamer
5. La crèmerie nf | The creamery
6. La crème fraîche nf | The whipped cream
7. La crème anglaise nf | The custard
8. La crème solaire nf | The sunscreen

— *Je prends de la **crème** dans mon café* • I take cream with my coffee

CRIME

1. Un crime nm | A crime
2. Un criminel nm | A criminal
3. Une criminelle nf | A criminal
4. Criminel - Criminelle Adj | Criminal

— *Un **criminel** s'est échappé de la prison* • A criminal escaped from the prison

CRITIQUE

1. Une critique nf | Criticism
2. Critiquer v | To criticize
3. Critique Adj | Critical

— *Une **critique** peut être constructive* • Criticism can be constructive

CROIRE

1. Croire v | To believe
2. Une croix nf | A cross
3. Une croyance nf | A belief

— *Je **crois** qu'il a perdu son travail* • I believe he lost his job

CUISINE

1. La cuisine nf | The kitchen
2. Le cuisinier nm | The cook
3. La cuisinière nf | The cook
4. La cuisinière nf | The stove
5. Cuisiner v | To cook
6. La cuisson nf | The cooking
7. Le cuistot nm | The cook

— *La **cuisson** va prendre 2 heures* • The cooking will take 2 hours

Dd.

DAME

1. Une dame nf | A lady
2. Madame nf | Madam
3. Mademoiselle nf | Miss
4. Mesdames - Mesdemoiselles nf | Madam / Miss (Pl)

— *Une **dame** a déposé ce paquet pour toi* • A lady dropped this package for you

DANGER

1. Un danger nm | A danger
2. Dangereux - Dangereuse Adj | Dangerous
3. La dangerosité nf | The dangerousness
4. Dangereusement Adv | Dangerously

— *Cette route est **dangereuse** en hiver* • This road is dangerous in winter

DANSE

1. Une danse nf | A dance
2. Danser v | To dance
3. Un danseur nm | A dancer
4. Une danseuse nf | A dancer

— *Les **danseurs** s'entrainent tous les jours !* • Dancers work out every day!

DÉBAT

1. Un débat nm | A debate
2. Débattre v | To debate

— *Le **débat** télévisé entre les deux candidats aura lieu samedi* • The television debate between the two candidates will take place this Saturday

DÉBUT

1. Un début nm | A beginning
2. Débuter v | To begin
3. Un débutant nm | A beginner
4. Une débutante nf | A beginner

— *Le cours **débute** à 8 heures* • The course begins at 8 am

DÉCEVOIR

1. Décevoir v | To disappoint
2. Déçu - Déçue Adj | Disappointed
3. La déception nf | The disappointment
4. Décevant - Décevante Adj | Disappointing

— *Je suis **déçu** de ne pas pouvoir aller en vacances* • I am disappointed to not be able to go on vacation

DÉCIDER

1. Décider v | To decide
2. Une décision nf | A decision
3. Un décideur nm | A decision-maker

— *J'ai pris la **décision** de changer de travail* • I took the decision to change jobs

DÉCLARER

1. Déclarer v | To declare
2. Une déclaration nf | A declaration

— *Il **déclare** ses sentiments à sa petite-amie* • He declares his feelings to his girlfriend

DÉCOUVRIR

1. Découvrir v | To discover
2. Une découverte nf | A discovery
3. Un découvreur nm | A discoverer
4. Découvrant Adj | Discovering

— ***Découvrir** ses passions est fascinant* • Discovering your passions is fascinating

DÉCRIRE

1. Décrire v | To describe
2. Une description nf | A description
3. Descriptif - Descriptive Adj | Descriptive

— *La victime **décrit** le suspect à la police* • The victim describes the suspect to the police

DÉFENDRE

1. Défendre v | To defend
2. Défendu Adj | Defended
3. Le défenseur nm | The defender
4. Une défense nf | A defence

— La **défense** *expose les faits au juge* • The defense exposes the facts to the judge

DÉFINIR

1. Définir v | To define
2. Une définition nf | A definition

— La **définition** *d'un mot aide à mieux l'utiliser* • The definition of a word helps to use it better

DÉGOÛT

1. Le dégoût nm | The disgust
2. Dégoûter v | To disgust
3. Dégoûtant - Dégoûtant Adj | Disgusting

— *Le sol est* **dégoûtant**, *il est temps de faire le ménage* • The floor is disgusting, it's time to do some housework

DÉJÀ

1. Déjà Adv | Already
2. Un déjà-vu nm | A déjà-vu

— *Je viens d'avoir un incroyable* **déjà-vu** • I just got a crazy déjà-vu

DÉJEUNER

1. Déjeuner v | To have lunch
2. Le déjeuner nm | The lunch
3. Le petit déjeuner nm | The breakfast
4. Jeûner v | To fast

— *Je mange toujours des tartines au* **petit-déjeuner** • I always eat toast for breakfast

DEMANDER

1. Demander v | To ask / To request
2. Une demande nf | A request
3. Un demandeur nm | An applicant
4. Une demandeuse nf | An applicant

— *Il a **demandé** un meeting avec son patron* • He requested a meeting with his boss

DÉMARRER

1. Démarrer v | To start
2. Un démarrage nm | A start

— *La voiture ne **démarre** plus* • The car doesn't start anymore

DÉMÉNAGER

1. Déménager v | To move out
2. Un déménagement nm | A move
3. Un déménageur nm | A mover

— *Nous **déménageons** la semaine prochaine* • We are moving out next week

DÉMONTRER

1. Démontrer v | To demonstrate
2. Une démonstration nf | A demonstration

— *La **démonstration** de ce produit est très convaincante* • The demonstration of this product is very convincing

DENT

1. Une dent nf | A tooth
2. Un dentiste nm | A dentist
3. Une dentiste nf | A dentist
4. Une dent de lait nf | A baby tooth
5. Une dent de sagesse nf | A wisdom tooth
6. La dentition nf | The dentition
7. Le dentifrice nm | The toothpaste
8. Un dentier nm | A denture

9. La brosse à dents nf | The toothbrush
10. Dentaire Adj | Dental
11. Un appareil dentaire nm | A brace
— *Elle se fait enlever les **dents de sagesse** ce vendredi* • She gets her wisdom teeth removed this Friday

DÉPENDRE
1. Dépendre v | To depend
2. La dépendance nf | The dependence
3. L'indépendance nf | The independence
4. Dépendant - Dépendante Adj | Dependent
5. Indépendant - Indépendante Adj | Independent / Self employed
6. Dépendamment Adv | Dependently
7. Indépendamment Adv | Independently
— *Ce que l'on va faire ce week-end **dépend** du temps* • What we will do this weekend depends on the weather

DÉPENSER
1. Dépenser v | To spend
2. Une dépense nf | An expense
3. Dépensier - Dépensière Adj | Spender
— *Ma tante est **dépensière*** • My aunt is a spender

DÉRANGER
1. Déranger v | To disturb
2. Un dérangement nm | A disturbance
— *Merci de ne pas **déranger*** • Thanks to not disturb

DÉSERT
1. Un désert nm | A desert
2. Déserter v | To desert
3. Désertique Adj | Desert
4. Un déserteur nm | A deserter

—— *Il fait tellement chaud, le paysage est **désertique*** • It's so warm, the landscape is a desert

DÉSESPÉRER

1. Désespérer v | To despair
2. Le désespoir nm | The despair
3. Désespéré - Désespérée Adj | Desperate
4. Désespérant - Désespérante Adj | Hopeless

—— *Je **désepère** de voir un jour des koalas* • I am desperate to one day see koalas

DESIGN

1. Un design nm | A design
2. Un designer nm | A designer

—— *Le **design** de ce canapé est fantastique* • The design of this couch is fantastic

DÉSIR

1. Un désir nm | A desire
2. Désirer v | To desire
3. Désireux - Désireuse Adj | Willing

—— *Je **désire** me marier avant 35 ans* • I desire to get married before 35

DESSIN

1. Un dessin nm | A drawing
2. Dessiner v | To draw
3. Un dessinateur nm | A cartoonist
4. Une dessinatrice nf | A cartoonist
5. Une bande dessinée nf | A comic book
6. Un dessin animé nm | A cartoon

—— *La Belgique est connue pour ses **bandes dessinées*** • Belgium is known for its comic books

DÉTAIL

1. Un détail nm | A detail

2. Détailler v | To detail
3. Un détaillant nm | A retailer
4. Une détaillante nf | A retailer
— Les **détails** de ce tableau sont impressionnants • The details of this painting are impressive

DÉTECTER

1. Détecter v | To detect
2. La détection nf | The detection
3. Le détecteur de fumée nm | The smoke detector
4. Détectable Adj | Detectable
— Le **détecteur de fumée** sonne quand les piles sont vides • The smoke detector goes on when the batteries are empty

DÉTERMINE

1. Déterminer v | To determine
2. La détermination nf | The determination
3. Un déterminant nm | A determiner
— Il faut **déterminer** ce qui est nécessaire avant d'acheter • We need to determine what is necessary before buying

DÉTRUIRE

1. Détruire v | To destroy
2. Détruit Adj | Destroyed
3. La destruction nf | The destruction
— La vieille maison au bout de la rue va être **détruite** • The old house at the end of the street will be destroyed

DETTE

1. Une dette nf | A debt
2. Endetter v | To indebt
— Il s'est beaucoup **endetté** ces dernières années • He put himself in debt these last few years

DÉVELOPPER
1. Développer v | To develop
2. Le développement nm | The development

— *Le **développement** de ce quartier va prendre plusieurs années* • The development of this neighborhood will take several years

DEVOIR
1. Devoir v | To have to
2. Un devoir nm | A duty / A homework

— *Fais tes **devoirs** avant d'aller jouer* • Do your homework before going to play

DIALOGUE
1. Un dialogue nm | A dialogue
2. Dialoguer v | To dialogue / To talk

— ***Dialoguer** avec son époux est important* • Talking with your spouse is important

DIFFÉRENCE
1. Une différence nf | A difference
2. Différencier v | To differentiate
3. Différemment Adv | Differently
4. Différent - Différente Adj | Different

— *Nous avons une légère **différence** de taille* • We have a slight difference in height

DIFFICILE
1. Difficile Adj | Difficult
2. Une difficulté nf | A difficulty
3. Difficilement Adv | Hardly

— *C'est **difficile** de toujours manger sain* • It's difficult to always eat healthy

DIGÉRER
1. Digérer v | To digest

2. La digestion nf | The digestion

3. Une indigestion nf | An indigestion

4. Le système digestif nm | The digestive system

— *Je vais me promener pour **digérer*** • I am going for a walk to digest

DIMINUER

1. Diminuer v | To reduce

2. Une diminution nf | A reduction

— *Le **recyclage** diminue les déchets dans la nature* • Recycling decreases waste in nature

DÎNER

1. Le dîner nm | The dinner

2. Dîner v | To have dinner

— *Le **dîner** est prêt* •Dinner is ready

DIRECT

1. Direct - Directe Adj | Direct

2. La direction nf | The direction

3. Directement Adv | Directly

4. Le directeur nm | The director

5. La directrice nf | The director

— *La **direction** de la compagnie se réunit ce samedi* • The direction of the company meets this Saturday

DIRIGER

1. Diriger v | To direct

2. Un dirigeant nm | A leader

3. Une dirigeante nf | A leader

— *Le GPS nous **dirige** sur la mauvaise route* • The GPS directs us to the wrong road

DISCIPLINE

1. La discipline nf | The discipline

2. Discipliner v | To discipline

—— *Il faut beaucoup de **discipline** pour être entrepreneur* • You need a lot of discipline to be an entrepreneur

DISCRIMINER

1. Discriminer v | To discriminate
2. La discrimination nf | The discrimination

—— *La **discrimation** au sein de l'école est inadmissible* • Discrimination in the school is inadmissible

DISCUTER

1. Discuter v | To discuss
2. Discutable Adj | Questionable
3. Une discussion nf | A discussion

—— *Les résultats de cette entreprise sont **discutables*** • The results of this company are questionable

DISPARAÎTRE

1. Disparaître v | To disappear
2. Une disparition nf | A disappearance

—— *La **disparition** de cette personne est inquiétante* • The disappearance of this person is worrying

DISPONIBLE

1. Disponible Adj | Available
2. Une disponibilité nf | An availability

—— *Est-ce que ce produit est **disponible** ?* • Is this product available?

DISTANCE

1. La distance nf | The distance
2. Distancer v | To distance
3. Distant - Distante Adj | Distant

—— *La **distance** entre ces deux villes est de 15 kilomètres* • The distance between these two cities is 15 kilometers

DIVORCE

1. Le divorce nm | The divorce
2. Un divorcé nm | A divorced
3. Une divorcée nf | A divorced
4. Divorcer v | To divorce

— *Notre **divorce** est finalement terminé* • Our divorce is finally over

DOCUMENT

1. Un document nm | A document
2. Documenter v | To document
3. Un documentaire nm | A documentary
4. La documentation nf | The documentation

— *As-tu vu ce **documentaire** sur l'Afrique ?* • Have you seen this documentary about Africa?

DON

1. Un don nm | A donation
2. Donner v | To donate / To give
3. Un donneur nm | A donor
4. Une donation nf | A donation
5. Un donateur nm | A donor

— *Je **donne** tous les mois à la SPCA* • I donate every month to the SPCA

DOUBLE

1. Un double nm | A double
2. Double Adj | Double
3. Doubler v | To double
4. Une doublure nf | A lining
5. Un doublage nm | A dubbing
6. Redoubler v | To redouble
7. Dédoubler v | To duplicate

— *J'ai certainement payé le **double** du prix* • I certainly paid double the price

DOUCE

1. Doux - Douce Adj | Soft
2. La douceur nf | The softness
3. Doucement Adv | Softly
4. Adoucir v | To soften
5. Un adoucissant nm | A softener

— *Cette couverture est très **douce*** • This blanket is very soft

DOUCHE

1. Une douche nf | A shower
2. Se doucher v | To shower
3. Une douchette nf | A shower head
4. Un gel douche nm | A shower gel

— *Nous n'avons plus de **gel douche*** • We don't have any more shower gel

DOULEUR

1. Une douleur nf | A pain
2. Douloureux - Douloureuse Adj | Painful
3. Douloureusement Adv | Painfully

— *Mon genou est **douloureux** après une course* • My knee is painful after a race

DRAME

1. Un drame nm | A drama
2. Dramatique Adj | Dramatic

— *Il y a tellement de **drames** dans cette série télévisée* • There is so much drama in this TV show

DROITE

1. La droite nf | Right
2. Un droitier nm | A right-handed
3. Une droitière nf | A right-handed

— *Es-tu **droitier** ou gaucher ?* • Are you right-handed or left-handed?

DUR

1. **Dur - Dure** Adj | Hard
2. **Durer** v | To last
3. **Durable** Adj | Durable
4. **La durée** nf | The duration

—— *La présentation devrait **durer** une heure* • The presentation should last an hour

Ee.

ÉCHAPPER

1. Échapper v | To escape
2. Un pot d'échappement nm | An exhaust
3. Une échappatoire nf | A loophole
4. Une échappée nf | An escape

— *Le prisonnier s'est **échappé** de la prison* • The prisoner escaped from jail

ÉCOLE

1. Une école nf | A school
2. Un écolier nm | A student
3. Une écolière nf | A student

— *L'**école** fini tous les jours à 15 heures* • School finishes every day at 3 pm

ÉCONOME

1. Économe Adj | Economical
2. Économiser v | To save
3. Des économies nf | Savings

— *Mes **économies** augmentent tous les mois* • My savings increase every month

ÉCRIRE

1. Écrire v | To write
2. Un écrivain nm | An author
3. Une écrivaine nf | An author
4. Une écriture nf | A writing

— *L'**écrivain** souffre de la page blanche* • The author suffers from writer's block

ÉDUQUER

1. Éduquer v | To educate
2. Une éducation nf | An education
3. Éducatif - Éducative Adj | Educational
4. Un éducateur nm | An educator

5. Une éducatrice nf | An educator

— *Ce programme **éducatif** est très bien pour les enfants* • This educational program is very good for children

ÉGOÏSTE

1. Égoïste Adj | Selfish
2. L'égoïsme nm | Selfishness
3. Égoïstement Adv | Selfishly

— *C'est **égoïste** de ne pas partager* • It's selfish not to share

ÉLECTRICITÉ

1. L'électricité nf | The electricity
2. Électrique Adj | Electrical
3. Un électricien nm | An electrician
4. Une électricienne nf | An electrician
5. Électrocuter v | To electrocute
6. Un électroménager nm | An appliance
7. Électronique Adj | Electronic

— *L'**électricien** devrait venir cet après-midi* • The electrician should come this afternoon

ÉLIMINER

1. Éliminer v | To eliminate
2. Une élimination nf | An elimination
3. Un éliminatoire nm | A qualifier / A playoff

— ***Éliminer** le plastique est important pour la planète* • Eliminating plastic is important for the planet

EMBRAYER

1. Embrayer v | To put into gear
2. Un embrayage nm | A clutch

— *La voiture a besoin d'un nouvel **embrayage*** • The car needs a new clutch

ÉMOTION

1. Une émotion nf | An emotion
2. Émotif - Émotive Adj | Emotional
3. Émouvant - Émouvante Adj | Moving
— *Leur mariage était très **émouvant*** • Their wedding was really moving

EMPLOYER

1. Employer v | To employ
2. Un emploi nm | An employment
3. Un employé nm | An employee
4. Une employée nf | An employee
— *Ma société **emploie** 10 personnes* • My society employs 10 people

EMPRUNT

1. Un emprunt nm | A loan
2. Emprunter v | To borrow
3. Un emprunteur nm | A borrower
— *Mon **emprunt** devrait être payé l'année prochaine* • My loan should be paid by next year

ENCOURAGER

1. Encourager v | To encourage
2. Un encouragement nm | An encouragement
— *Il **encourage** toujours ses élèves* • He always encourages his students

ENFANT

1. Un enfant nm | A child
2. L'enfance nf | The childhood
3. Enfantin Adj | Childish
— *Ils ont 3 **enfants** ensemble* • They have 3 children together

ENNUYER

1. Ennuyer v | To bother
2. S'ennuyer v | To be bored

3. L'ennui nm | The boredom
4. Ennuyeux - Ennuyeuse Adj | Boring
— *Ce film est **ennuyeux*** • This movie is boring

ENQUÊTE
1. Une enquête nf | An investigation
2. Enquêter v | To investigate
3. Un enquêteur nm | An investigator
4. Une enquêtrice nf | An investigator
— *L'**enquête** pour fraude est toujours en cours* • The investigation for fraud is still on

ENSEIGNER
1. Enseigner v | To teach
2. Un enseignant nm | A teacher
3. Une enseignante nf | A teacher
4. Un enseignement nm | An education
— *Être **enseignant** est un métier difficile* •Being a teacher is a difficult job

ENTERRER
1. Enterrer v | To bury
2. Un enterrement nm | A funeral
3. La terre nf | The soil
4. Un enterrement de vie de garçon nm | A bachelor party
5. Un enterrement de vie de jeune fille nm | A bachelorette party
— *L'**enterrement** aura lieu dans la plus stricte intimité* • The funeral will take place in strict privacy

ENTHOUSIASTE
1. Enthousiaste Adj | Enthusiastic
2. Un enthousiasme nm | An enthusiasm
— *Son **enthousiasme** est contagieux* • His enthusiasm is contagious

ENTRER

1. Entrer v | To enter
2. L'entrée nf | The entrance
— *Laisse ton manteau dans l'entrée s'il te plaît* • Leave your coat by the entrance please

ENVOI

1. Un envoi nm | A mailing
2. Envoyer v | To send
— *J'ai envoyé mes cartes de Noël hier soir* • I sent my Christmas cards yesterday evening

ÉPAULE

1. Une épaule nf | A shoulder
2. Épauler v | To support
3. Les épaulettes nf | The epaulettes
— *Le manager est épaulé par son assistant* • The manager is supported by his assistant

ÉPILER

1. Épiler v | To pluck
2. Une épilation nf | A hair removal
3. La pince à épiler nf | The tweezers
— *J'ai rendez-vous avec mon esthéticienne pour une épilation* • I have an appointment with my esthetician for hair removal

ÉPOUSE

1. Un époux nm | A spouse
2. Une épouse nf | A spouse
3. Épouser v | To marry
— *Mon époux a sa propre compagnie* • My spouse has his own company

ÉQUIPE

1. Une équipe nf | A team
2. Équiper v | To equip

3. Un équipement nm | An equipment
— *Cette **équipe** de rugby est très soudée* • This rugby team is very united

ESPACE

1. L'espace nm | The space
2. Espacer v | To space
— *Les États-Unis envoient un nouveau satellite dans l'**espace*** •
The United-States sends a new satellite into space

ESPÉRER

1. Espérer v | To hope
2. L'espérance nf | The hope
3. L'espoir nm | The hope
4. L'espérance de vie nf | The life expectancy
— *J'**espère** que tu vas bien* • I hope you are doing well

ESSAYER

1. Essayer v | To try
2. Un essai nm | A test
3. Un essayage nm | A fitting
— *Je vais **essayer** ce pantalon* • I am going to try on these pants

ESSENTIEL

1. Un essentiel nm | An essential
2. Essentiel - Essentielle Adj | Essential
3. Essentiellement Adv | Essentially
4. Une huile essentielle nf | An essential oil
— *Les **huiles essentielles** sont à utiliser avec précaution* • Essential
oils have to be used with precaution

ESSUIE

1. Un essuie nm | A towel
2. Un essuie-mains nm | A hand towel
3. Un essuie-tout nm | A paper towel
4. Un essuie-glace nm | A wipers

5. Essuyer v | To wipe
— *Les **essuie-glaces** sont vieux, il faut les changer* • The wipers are old, they need to be changed

ESTHÉTIQUE
1. Esthétique Adj | Aesthetic
2. Une esthéticienne nf | An esthetician
3. Un salon esthétique nm | A beauty salon
4. Un chirurgien esthétique nm | A plastic surgeon
— *Le **chirurgien esthétique** travaille souvent avec les grands brûlés* • The plastic surgeon often works with the burns unit

ÉTINCÈLE
1. Une étincèle nf | A spark
2. Étinceler v | To sparkle
3. Étincelant - Étincelante Adj | Sparkling
— *Le sapin de Noël est **étincelant*** •The Christmas tree is sparkling

ÉVALUER
1. Évaluer v | To evaluate
2. Une évaluation nf | An evaluation
3. Un évaluateur nm | An evaluator
4. Une évaluatrice nf | An evaluator
— *Il faut **évaluer** les pour et les contre avant de prendre une décision* • You need to evaluate the pros and cons before making a decision

ÉVOLUER
1. Évoluer v | To evolve
2. Une évolution nf | An evolution
— *Les scientifiques étudient l'**évolution** de la planète* • The scientists study the evolution of the planet

EXACT
1. Exact - Exacte Adj | Exact
2. Exactement Adv | Exactly

3. Une exactitude nf | An accuracy

— *C'est **exactement** ce que j'ai répondu* • It's exactly what I answered

EXAMINER

1. Examiner v | To examine
2. Un examen nm | An exam
3. Un examinateur nm | An examiner
4. Une examinatrice nf | An examiner

— *Il a réussi son **examen** avec succès* • He passed his exam with success

EXCELLER

1. Exceller v | To excel
2. Excellent - Excellente Adj | Excellent
3. Une excellence nf | An excellence

— *Ce gâteau est **excellent*** • This cake is excellent

EXERCICE

1. Un exercice nm | An exercise
2. S'exercer v | To exercise

— *Il cherche un livre d'**exercices** de mathématiques* • He is looking for a mathematics exercise book

EXISTER

1. Exister v | To exist
2. Existant - Existante Adj | Existing
3. Une existence nf | An existence

— *Les fées n'**existent** pas dans le monde réel* • Fairies don't exist in the real world

EXPLIQUER

1. Expliquer v | To explain
2. Une explication nf | An explanation
3. Explicatif - Explicative Adj | Explanatory

— Les **explications** de ce produit sont très claires • The explanations of this product are very clear

EXPLORER

1. Explorer v | To explore
2. Une exploration nf | An exploration
3. Un explorateur nm | An explorer
4. Une exploratrice nf | An explorer

— C'est un bon point de départ pour **explorer** les environs • It's a good starting point to explore around

EXPLOSER

1. Exploser v | To explode
2. Une explosion nf | An explosion
3. Explosif - Explosive Adj | Explosive

— On pouvait entendre l'**explosion** sur plusieurs kilomètres • We could hear the explosion from a few kilometers away

EXPRIMER

1. Exprimer v | To express
2. Une expression nf | An expression
3. Expressif - Expressive Adj | Expressive

— **Exprimer** ses sentiments est important • Expressing his feelings is important

EXTRÊME

1. Extrême Adj | Extreme
2. Extrêmement Adv | Extremely

— Les sports **extrêmes** sont dangereux • Extreme sports are dangerous

Ff.

FAÇON

1. Une façon nf | A way
2. Façonner v | To shape

— *Sa **façon** de travailler est très productive* • His way of working is very productive

FACTURE

1. Une facture nf | An invoice / A bill
2. La facturation nf | The invoicing / The billing
3. Facturer v | To invoice / To bill

— *As-tu reçu la **facture** d'eau ?* • Did you get the water bill?

FAMILLE

1. La famille nf | The family
2. La belle-famille nf | The in-laws
3. Familier - Familière Adj | Familiar
4. Un nom de famille nm | A surname
5. Familiariser v | To familiarize

— *Ma **famille** habite en Belgique* • My family lives in Belgium

FATIGUE

1. La fatigue nf | The fatigue
2. Fatiguer v | To tire
3. Fatigué - Fatiguée Adj | Tired
4. Fatigant - Fatigante Adj | Tiring

— *Je suis toujours **fatiguée** le week-end* • I am always tired on the weekend

FÉLICITER

1. Féliciter v | To congratulate
2. Des félicitations nf | Congratulations

— ***Félicite** le pour moi quand tu le vois* • Congratulate him for me when you see him

FERME
1. Une ferme nf | A farm
2. Un fermier nm | A farmer
3. Une fermière nf | A farmer
— *La **ferme** vend ses propres légumes* • The farm sells its own vegetables

FERMER
1. Fermer v | To close
2. La fermeture nf | The closure
3. Une fermeture éclair nf | A zipper
— ***Ferme** la porte derrière toi* • Close the door behind you

FERTILE
1. Fertile Adj | Fertile
2. La fertilité nf | The fertility
3. Fertiliser v | To fertilize
4. Un fertilisant nm | A fertilizer
5. La fertilisation nf | The fertilization
6. Infertile Adj | Infertile
7. L'infertilité nf | The infertility
— *L'**infertilité** est un problème courant chez les personnes de plus de 30 ans* • Infertility is a common problem for people over 30 years old

FIANCÉ
1. Un fiancé nm | A fiancé
2. Une fiancée nf | A fiancée
3. Se fiancer v | To become engaged
4. Les fiançailles nf | The engagement
— *Nous sommes **fiancés** depuis le mois dernier* • We have been engaged since last month

FIER
1. Fier - Fière Adj | Proud
2. La fierté nf | The pride

3. Fièrement Adv | Proudly

— *Nous sommes **fiers** de toi et de tes progrès* • We are proud of you and your progress

FIGUE

1. Une figue nf | A fig
2. Un figuier nm | A fig tree

— *La **figue** est riche en vitamines* • The fig is rich in vitamins

FILM

1. Un film nm | A film
2. Filmer v | To film
3. La filmographie nf | The filmography

— *Ce **film** est une œuvre d'art !* • This movie is a work of art!

FINAL

1. Final - Finale Adj | Final
2. La finale nf | The finale
3. Finaliser v | To finalize
4. La finalisation nf | The finalization
5. Finalement Adv | Finally

— *La **finale** du championnat commence samedi* • The championship finale starts on Saturday

FINANCE

1. La finance nf | The finance
2. Un financement nm | A funding
3. Financer v | To finance
4. Financièrement Adv | Financially

— *J'ai obtenu un **financement** pour mes rénovations* • I got financing for my renovations

FIXE

1. Fixe Adj | Permanent
2. Fixer v | To fix / To hang

3. Une fixation nf | A fixation

— *Il a **fixé** le tableau au mur* • He hung the painting on the wall

FLEUR

1. Une fleur nf | A flower
2. Fleurir v | To bloom
3. Un fleuriste nm | A florist
4. Une fleuriste nf | A florist

— *J'ai reçu un magnifique bouquet de **fleurs*** • I got a beautiful bouquet of flowers

FONCTION

1. Une fonction nm | A function
2. Fonctionner v | To work
3. Un fonctionnement nm | An operation
4. La fonctionnalité nf | The functionality

— *Le four ne **fonctionne** plus depuis hier* • The oven hasn't been working since yesterday

FONDER

1. Fonder v | To establish
2. Un fondement nm | A foundation
3. Une fondation nf | A foundation
4. Fondamental - Fondamentale Adj | Fundamental
5. Un fondateur nm | A founder
6. Une fondatrice nf | A founder

— *Il est **fondamental** de prendre soin de soi* • It's fundamental to take care of yourself

FORMER

1. Former v | To form
2. Une formation nf | A training
3. Un formateur nm | A trainer
4. Une formatrice nf | A trainer

— *Je participe à une **formation** sur la publicité* • I'm participating in training for advertising

FORT

1. Fort - Forte Adj | Strong
2. Fortement Adv | Strongly

— *Ce café est très **fort*** • This coffee is very strong

FOULER

1. Se fouler v | To sprain
2. Une foulure nf | A sprain

— *Il ne peut pas marcher car il s'est **foulé** la cheville* • He can't walk because he sprained his ankle

FOUR

1. Un four nm | An oven
2. Une fournée nf | A batch
3. Enfourner v | To place in the oven

— *Le gâteau est dans le **four** pour 40 minutes* • The cake is in the oven for 40 minutes

FRACTURE

1. Une fracture nf | A fracture
2. Fracturer v | To fracture
3. Une fracturation nf | A fracturing

— *Il s'est **fracturé** la jambe en tombant à vélo* • He fractured his leg falling from his bike

FRAÎCHE

1. Frais - Fraîche Adj | Fresh
2. La fraîcheur nf | The freshness
3. Fraîchement Adv | Freshly
4. Rafraîchir v | To refresh
5. Un rafraîchissement nm | A refreshment

— *Les légumes de ce magasin sont toujours **frais*** • Vegetables from this shop are always fresh

FRAISE
1. Une fraise nf | A strawberry
2. Un fraisier nm | A strawberry plant
— *La saison des **fraises** commence le mois prochain* • Strawberry season starts next month

FRAMBOISE
1. Une framboise nf | A raspberry
2. Un framboisier nm | A raspberry bush
— *Cette confiture à la **framboise** est délicieuse* • This raspberry jam is delicious

FREIN
1. Un frein nm | A brake
2. Freiner v | To brake
3. Le freinage nm | The braking
4. Une plaquette de frein nf | A brake pad
— *Les **freins** servent à arrêter un véhicule* • Brakes are used to stop a vehicle

FRÉQUENT
1. Fréquent - Fréquente Adj | Frequent
2. Fréquemment Adv | Frequently
3. Une fréquence nf | A frequency
4. Fréquenter v | To frequent
— *Je voyage en Europe **fréquemment*** • I travel to Europe frequently

FRUIT
1. Un fruit nm | A fruit
2. Un jus de fruit nm | A fruit juice
3. Fruitier - Fruitière Adj | Fruit
4. Les fruits de mer nm | Seafood

— *Nous aimerions avoir un arbre **fruitier** dans le jardin* • We would like to have a fruit tree in the yard

FRUSTRER

1. Frustrer v | To frustrate
2. La frustration nf | The frustration
3. Frustrant - Frustrante Adj | Frustrating

— *C'est **frustrant** de ne pas être au niveau que l'on veut* • It's frustrating to not be at the level we want

FROID

1. Le froid nm | The cold
2. Froid - Froide Adj | Cold
3. Refroidir v | To cool
4. Un refroidissement nm | A cooling
5. Froidement Adv | Coldly
6. La froideur nf | The coldness

— *Le mois de novembre est souvent un mois **froid*** • The month of November is usually a cold month

FRONT

1. Le front nm | The front / The forehead
2. La frontière nf | The border
3. Frontal - Frontale Adj | Frontal

— *Il a développé une allergie sur le **front*** • He developed an allergy on his forehead

FUMER

1. Fumer v | To smoke
2. Un fumeur nm | A smoker
3. Une fumeuse nf | A smoker
4. La fumée nf | The smoke

— ***Fumer** est une habitude nocive* • Smoking is a harmful habit

Gg.

GAGNER

1. Gagner v | To win
2. Un gagnant nm | A winner
3. Une gagnante nf | A winner
4. Un gain nm | A gain / A profit
— *Cette compagnie a réalisé un **gain** de 2 millions* • This company made a profit of 2 million

GALANT

1. Galant - Galante Adj | Gallant
2. La galanterie nf | The gallantry
— *Mon gendre est toujours **galant*** • My son-in-law is always gallant

GARDE

1. Un garde nm | A guard
2. Garder v | To keep
3. Un garde-manger nm | A pantry
4. Une mise en garde nf | A warning
5. Une page de garde nf | A cover
6. Un garde-corps nm | A guard rail
7. Une garderie nf | A daycare
— *Le **garde-manger** est rempli de boîtes de conserve* • The pantry is full of cans

GARNIR

1. Garnir v | To garnish
2. La garniture nf | The garnish / The decoration
3. Le garnissage nm | The garnishing
— *La **garniture** du gâteau est magnifique* • The decoration of the cake is beautiful

GAUCHE

1. La gauche nf | Left
2. Un gaucher nm | A left-handed
3. Une gauchère nf | A left-handed

4. Gauchement Adv | Awkwardly

— *Le magasin sera sur votre **gauche** au bout de la rue* • The shop will be on your left at the end of the street

GÉNÉRAL

1. Général - Générale Adj | General
2. Généralement Adv | Generally
3. Une généralité nf | A generality

— ***Généralement** la livraison prend 3-4 jours* • Generally the delivery takes 3-4 days

GÉNÉREUX

1. Généreux - Généreuse Adj | Generous
2. Généreusement Adv | Generously
3. La générosité nf | The generosity

— *Il a donné une somme **généreuse** à cette association* • He gave a generous sum to this association

GENOU

1. Un genou nm | A knee
2. S'agenouiller v | To kneel
3. Une genouillère nm | A knee protector

— *N'oublie pas tes **genouillères** avant de faire du patin* • Don't forget your knees protectors before skating

GENTIL

1. Gentil - Gentille Adj | Kind
2. La gentillesse nf | The kindness
3. Gentiment Adv | Kindly

— *C'est très **gentil** de ta part* • It's very kind of you

GLACE

1. La glace nf | The ice
2. Un glaçon nm | An ice cube
3. Un glacier nm | A glacier

4. Glacer v | To ice
5. Une glacière nf | A cooler
6. Une crème glacée nf | An ice cream
7. Le sucre glace nm | The icing sugar

— *La **crème glacée** au chocolat est ma préférée* • Chocolate ice cream is my favourite

GLOBE

1. Un globe nm | A globe
2. Global - Globale Adj | Global
3. Globalement Adv | Globally
4. Un globule blanc nm | A white blood cell
5. Un globule rouge nm | A red blood cell

— *Le professeur a acheté un **globe** pour la classe* • The teacher bought a globe for the classroom

GORGE

1. La gorge nf | The throat
2. Un mal de gorge nm | A sore throat
3. Une gorgée nf | A sip
4. Un rouge-gorge nm | A robin
5. Un soutien-gorge nm | A bra

— *As-tu vu le **rouge-gorge** sur le balcon ?* • Have you seen the robin on the balcony?

GOÛT

1. Le goût nm | The taste
2. Goûter v | To taste
3. Un goûter nm | A snack

— *Il faut **goûter** ce que l'on cuisine* • You need to taste what you cook

GRAND

1. Grand - Grande Adj | Tall / Large
2. La grandeur nf | The size
3. Grandement Adv | Largely

79

4. Grandir v | To grow up

— *Il **grandit** tellement vite !* • He grows up so fast!

GRÊLE

1. La grêle nf | The hail
2. Grêler v | To hail

— *Il va certainement **grêler** demain* • It will certainly hail tomorrow

GUIDE

1. Un guide nm | A guide
2. Guider v | To guide
3. Un guide touristique nm | A tour guide
4. Un chien guide nm | A guide dog

— *Un **chien guide** est nécessaire pour les aveugles* • A guide dog is necessary for blind people

GYMNASTIQUE

1. La gymnastique nf | The gymnastic
2. Un gymnaste nm | A gymnast
3. Une gymnaste nf | A gymnast

— *Elle aimerait devenir **gymnaste*** • She would like to become a gymnast

Hh.

HABITER

1. Habiter v | To live
2. Une habitation nf | A home
3. Un habitat nm | A habitat
4. Un habitant nm | A resident
5. Une habitante nf | A resident
   — *Nous **habitons** à la campagne* • We live in the countryside

HABITUDE

1. Une habitude nf | An habit
2. Habituer v | To use to
3. Habituel - Habituelle Adj | Usual
4. Habituellement Adv | Usually
   — ***Habituellement** je mange 3 repas par jour* • Usually I eat 3 times a day

HAUT

1. Haut - Haute Adj | High
2. La hauteur nf | The height
3. Hautement Adv | Highly
4. Hautain - Hautaine Adj | Arrogant
   — *La **hauteur** du building est de 25 mètres* • The height of the building is 25 meters

HERBE

1. Une herbe nf | An herb
2. Un herbivore nm | An herbivore
3. Un herbier nm | An herbarium
   — *Les vaches sont **herbivores*** • Cows are herbivore

HÉRITER

1. Hériter v | To inherit
2. Un héritier nm | An heir
3. Une héritière nf | An heiress

4. Un héritage nm | An inheritance

— *L'**héritage** devrait être finalisé la semaine prochaine* • The inheritance should be finalized next week

HÉROS

1. Un héros nm | A hero
2. Une héroïne nf | A heroine
3. L'héroïsme nm | The heroism
4. Héroïque Adj | Heroic

— *Cet homme est un **héros*** • This man is a hero

HEUREUX

1. Heureux - Heureuse Adj | Happy
2. Heureusement Adv | Happily

— *Ils sont **heureux** dans leur mariage* • They are happy in their marriage

HISTOIRE

1. Une histoire nf | A story
2. L'Histoire nf | History
3. Historique Adj | Historic
4. Historiquement Adv | Historically
5. Un historien nm | An historian
6. Une historienne nf | An historian

— *Les enfants veulent une **histoire** avant de dormir* • Kids want a story before bedtime

HIVER

1. Un hiver nm | Winter
2. Hivernal - Hivernale Adj | Wintery

— *Cet **hiver** a été très dur* • This winter was really hard

HOMME

1. Un homme nm | A man
2. Un Homme nm | A human
3. Un bonhomme nm | A little man

4. Un bonhomme de neige nm | A snowman

— *Cet **homme** est le principal suspect* • This man is the main suspect

HONNÊTE

1. Honnête Adj | Honest
2. Honnêtement Adv | Honestly
3. L'honnêteté nf | The honesty

— ***Honnêtement,** le pantalon te va mieux* • Honestly, the pants suit you better

HONTE

1. La honte nf | Shame
2. Honteux - Honteuse Adj | Shameful

— *C'est **honteux** d'abandonner un animal* • It's shameful to abandon an animal

Ii.

IDENTITÉ

1. Une identité nf | An identity
2. Identifier v | To identify
3. Une identification nf | An identification
4. Indentifiable Adj | Identifiable

— *La victime a été **identifiée** rapidement* • The victim was identified quickly

ILLUSTRER

1. Illustrer v | To illustrate
2. Un illustrateur nm | An illustrator
3. Une illustratrice nf | An illustrator
4. Une illustration nf | An illustration

— *J'ai dessiné une **illustration** pour mon projet* • I drew an illustration for my project

IMMATRICULER

1. Immatriculer v | To register
2. Une immatriculation nf | A registration
3. Une plaque d'immatriculation nf | A license plate

— *La voiture est **immatriculée** en Allemagne* • The car is registered in Germany

IMMÉDIAT

1. Immédiat - Immédiate Adj | Instant
2. Immédiatement Adv | Immediatly

— *Elle a vu **immédiatement** que quelque chose n'allait pas* • She saw immediately that something wasn't right

IMMIGRER

1. Immigrer v | To immigrate
2. Un immigré nm | An immigrant
3. Une immigrée nf | An immigrant
4. Un immigrant nm | An immigrant
5. Une immigrante nf | An immigrant

6. L'immigration nf | The immigration

— *Chaque pays a un quota d'immigration* • Every country has a quota for immigration

IMPACT

1. Un impact nm | An impact
2. Impacter v | To impact

— *Ce projet aura un grand **impact** sur la communauté* • This project will have a big impact on the community

IMPLIQUER

1. Impliquer v | To involve
2. Une implication nf | An involvement

— *Toute la famille est **impliquée** dans les préparations de Noël* • The whole family is involved with Christmas preparations

IMPORTANT

1. Important - Importante Adj | Important
2. L'importance nf | The importance

— *C'est **important** de connaître la grammaire* • It's important to know grammar

IMPRESSION

1. Une impression nf | An impression
2. Impressionner v | To impress
3. Impressionnant - Impressionnante Adj | Impressive

— *Tes résultats sont **impressionnants*** • Your results are impressive

IMPRIMER

1. Imprimer v | To print
2. Une imprimante nf | A printer
3. Une imprimerie nf | A printing
4. Un imprimeur nm | A printer

— *L'**imprimante** ne fonctionne plus* • The printer doesn't work

INDÉPENDANCE

1. L'indépendance nf | The independence

2. Indépendant - Indépendant Adj | Independent

3. Un indépendant nm | A self-employed person

4. Une indépendante nf | A self-employed person

5. Indépendamment Adv | Independently

— *Les adolescents doivent s'habituer à être* **indépendants** • Adolescents have to get used to being independent

INDEX

1. Un index nm | An index

2. Indexer v | To index

3. L'indexation nf | The indexing

— **L'index** *d'un livre est utile pour trouver ce que l'on cherche* • The index of a book is useful to find what you are looking for

INDIQUER

1. Indiquer v | To indicate

2. Une indication nf | An indication

3. Un indicateur nm | An indicator

4. Une indicatrice nf | An indicator

5. Indicatif - Indicative Adj | Indicative

— *Veuillez* **indiquer** *si vous êtes enceinte* • Please indicate if you are pregnant

INDUSTRIE

1. Une industrie nf | An industry

2. Industriel - Industrielle Adj | Industrial

3. Une industrialisation nf | An industrialization

— **L'industrie** *du lait a perdu beaucoup de profit* • The milk industry lost a lot of profit

INFECTER

1. Infecter v | To infect

2. Une infection nf | An infection

— *La plaie est **infectée*** • The wound is infected

INFIRMIER

1. Un infirmier nm | A nurse
2. Une infirmière nf | A nurse
3. Une infirmerie nf | An infirmary

— *Il étudie pour devenir **infirmier*** • He is studying to become a nurse

INFLUENCE

1. Une influence nf | An influence
2. Influencer v | To influence
3. Influent - Influente Adj | Influential

— *Il a beaucoup d'**influence** sur son frère* • He has a lot of influence on his brother

INFORMER

1. Informer v | To inform
2. Une information nf | An information
3. Un informateur nm | An informer
4. Une informatrice nf | An informer

— *Cette **information** est cruciale pour l'entreprise* • This information is crucial for the company

INGÉNIEUR

1. Un ingénieur nm | An engineer
2. L'ingénierie nf | The engineering
3. Ingénieux - Ingénieuse Adj | Ingenious
4. Ingénieusement Adv | Ingeniously
5. Une ingéniosité nf | An ingenuity

— *J'ai un diplôme en **ingénierie*** • I have a degree in engineering

INITIALE

1. Une initiale nf | An initial
2. Initial - Initiale Adj | Initial

3. Initialement Adv | Initially

— *C'est notre plan initial* • It's our initial plan

INITIER

1. Initier v | To initiate

2. Une initiative nf | An initiative

— *Le nouvel employé prend de très bonnes initiatives* • The new employee takes very good initiatives

INNOCENT

1. Un innocent nm | An innocent

2. Une innocente nf | An innocent

3. Innocenter v | To clear / To find innocent

4. Innocent - Innocente Adj | Innocent

5. L'innocence nf | The innocence

— *Le prisonnier est innocent* • The prisoner is innocent

INSOLENT

1. Insolent - Insolente Adj | Insolent

2. L'insolence nf | The insolence

— *L'insolence est une partie de l'enfance* • Insolence is a part of childhood

INSTITUT

1. Un institut nm | An institute

2. Une institution nf | An institution

3. Un instituteur nm | A teacher

4. Une institutrice nf | A teacher

5. Institutionnel - Institutionnelle Adj | Institutional

6. Instituer v | To institute

— *Notre instituteur part à la retraite cette année* • Our teacher is leaving for retirement this year

INSTRUIRE

1. Instruire v | To educate
2. Instruit - Instruite Adj | Trained
3. Un instructeur nm | An instructor
4. Une instructrice nf | An instructor
5. Une instruction nf | An instruction
6. Instructif - Instructive Adj | Informative

— *L'école **instruit** les élèves* • The school educates students

INTENSE

1. Intense Adj | Intense
2. Intensément Adv | Intensely
3. L'intensité nf | Intensity

— *Ce café est **intense*** • This coffee is intense

INTERDIRE

1. Interdire v | To ban
2. Une interdiction nf | A ban
3. Interdit - Interdite Adj | Banned

— *Il a **interdiction** d'utiliser son iPad* • He has a ban from using his iPad

INTÉRÊT

1. Un intérêt nm | An interest
2. Intéresser v | To interest
3. Intéressant - Intéressante Adj | Interesting

— *C'est dans son **intérêt** d'apprendre le français* • It's in his own interest to learn French

INTERPRÈTE

1. Un interprète nm | An interpreter
2. Une interprète nf | An interpreter
3. Une interprétation nf | An interpretation
4. Interpréter v | To interpret

— *Son **interprétation** du livre était parfaite* • His interpretation of the book was perfect

INTERVENIR

1. Intervenir v | To intervene
2. Une intervention nf | An intervention
3. Un intervenant nm | An intervenor
4. Une intervenante nf | An intervenor

— *Il faut **intervenir** avant qu'il soit trop tard* • It's necessary to intervene before it's too late

INTIME

1. Intime Adj | Intimate
2. L'intimité nf | The privacy / The intimacy
3. Un journal intime nm | A diary

— *Un couple a besoin d'**intimité*** • A couple needs privacy

INTRODUIRE

1. Introduire v | To introduce
2. Une introduction nf | An introduction

— *L'**introduction** du livre est plus longue que prévue* • The book's introduction is longer than expected

INVENTER

1. Inventer v | To invent
2. Une invention nf | An invention
3. Un inventeur nm | An inventor
4. Une inventrice nf | An inventor

— *L'**inventeur** du saxophone est Alphonse Saxo* • The inventor of the saxophone is Alphonse Saxo

INVESTIR

1. Investir v | To invest
2. Un investisseur nm | An investor
3. Une investisseuse nf | An investor

4. Un investissement nm | An investment

— *Les actions sont des **investissements** risqués* • Stocks are risky investments

IRRITER

1. Irriter v | To irritate
2. Irritant - Irritante Adj | Irritating
3. Une irritation nf | An irritation

— *Le bébé a une **irritation** dans le dos* • The baby has an irritation on their back

Jj.

JALOUSE
1. Jaloux - Jalouse Adj | Jealous
2. La jalousie nf | The jealousy
3. Jalouser v | To envy
— La **jalousie** peut être négative pour un couple • Jealousy can be negative for a couple

JAMBE
1. Une jambe nf | A leg
2. Un jambon nm | A ham
3. Une jambe de bois nf | A wooden leg
4. Enjamber v | To span
— Il s'est cassé la **jambe** hier soir • He broke his leg yesterday evening

JARDIN
1. Un jardin nm | A garden
2. Jardiner v | To garden
3. Un jardinier nm | A gardener
4. Une jardinière nf | A gardener
5. Le jardinage nm | The gardening
— Ma belle-mère adore **jardiner** • My mother-in-law loves gardening

JET
1. Un jet nm | A jet
2. Jeter v | To throw
3. Jetable Adj | Disposable
— Les lingettes **jetables** sont nocives pour l'environnement • Disposable wipes are harmful for the environment

JEUNE
1. Un jeune nm | A young person
2. Une jeune nf | A young person
3. Jeune Adj | Young
4. La jeunesse nf | The youth
5. Une auberge de jeunesse nf | An hostel

— *Le **jeune** chien apprend à marcher en laisse* • The young dog is learning to walk on leash

JOUER

1. Jouer v | To play
2. Un joueur nm | A player
3. Une joueuse nf | A player
4. Un jouet nm | A toy
5. Un jeu nm | A game
   — *Veux-tu **jouer** aux cartes ?* • Do you want to play cards?

JOUR

1. Un jour nm | A day
2. Une journée nf | A day
   — *Les **journées** sont courtes en décembre* • Days are short in December

JOURNAL

1. Un journal nm | A newspaper
2. Un journal télévisé nm | TV news
3. Un journaliste nm | A journalist
4. Une journaliste nf | A journalist
   — *Mes parents regardent le **journal télévisé** tous les jours* • My parents watch the news on TV everyday

JOYEUX

1. Joyeux - Joyeuse Adj | Happy
2. Joyeusement Adv | Happily
3. La joie nf | The joy
4. Joyeuses fêtes | Happy holidays
   — *Elle était tellement **joyeuse** de te voir* • She was so happy to see you

JUDO

1. Le judo nm | The judo
2. Un judoka nm | A judoka
   — *Il a cours de **judo** tous les mardis* • He has judo every Tuesday

JUGE

1. Un juge nm | A judge
2. Une juge nf | A judge
3. Juger v | To judge
4. Un jugement nm | A judgment

— *Le **juge** l'a condamné à 2 ans de prison* • The judge condemned him to 2 years in prison

JUMELER

1. Jumeler v | To twin
2. Des jumeaux nm | Twins
3. Des jumelles nf | Twins
4. Un jumelage nm | A twinning

— *Mes sœurs aînées sont **jumelles*** • My oldest sisters are twins

JUSTE

1. Juste Adj | Just / Correct
2. La justice nf | The justice
3. Un palais de justice nm | A courthouse
4. Un huissier de justice nm | A court bailiff

— *Je trouve que la sentence était **juste*** • I think the sentence was correct

JUSTIFIER

1. Justifier v | To justify
2. Un justificatif nm | An evidence / A proof
3. Justificatif - Justificative Adj | Argumentative

— *En cas d'absence, merci d'apporter un **justificatif*** • In cases of absence, thanks for bringing a proof

Kk.

KLAXON

1. Un klaxon nm | A horn
2. Klaxonner v | To honk

— *Nous devrions utiliser le **klaxon** seulement en cas d'urgence* • We should use the horn only for emergencies

L1.

LACER

1. Lacer v | To lace / To tie
2. Un lacet nm | A shoelace
3. Le laçage nm | The lacing
   — *Fais tes **lacets** s'il te plaît* • Tie your shoelaces please

LÂCHER

1. Lâcher v | To release
2. Lâchement Adv | Cowardly
3. Lâche Adj | Coward
4. La lâcheté nf | Cowardliness
   — *Il a **lâchement** volé le sac d'une vieille dame* • He cowardly stole an old lady's purse

LANCER

1. Lancer v | To launch
2. Le lancement nm | The launch
   — *Le **lancement** du produit s'est déroulé parfaitement* • The launch of the product happened perfectly

LARGE

1. Large Adj | Wide
2. Largement Adv | Widely
3. La largeur nf | The width
   — *Ce pantalon est trop **large*** • This pair of pants is too wide

LAVER

1. Laver v | To wash
2. Lavable Adj | Washable
3. Un lavement nm | An enema
4. Le lavage nm | The wash
5. Une machine à laver nf | A washing machine
6. Un lave-vaisselle nm | A dishwasher

— *La **machine à laver** coule depuis ce matin* • The washing machine has been leaking since this morning

LÉGAL

1. Légal - Légale Adj | Legal
2. Légaliser v | To legalize
3. Légalement Adv | Legally
4. La légalisation nf | The legalization
5. Illégal - Illégale Adj | Illegal
6. Illégalement Adv | Illegally

— *C'est **illégal** de téléphoner en conduisant* • It's illegal to call while driving

LENT

1. Lent - lente Adj | Slow
2. La lenteur nf | The slowness
3. Lentement Adv | Slowly

— ***Lentement** mais sûrement* • Slowly but surely

LÈVRE

1. Une lèvre nf | A lip
2. Un rouge à lèvres nm | A lipstick

— *Je préfère un **rouge à lèvres** mat* • I prefer a matte lipstick

LIBÉRER

1. Libérer v | To free
2. La liberté nf | The liberty
3. La libération nf | The liberation
4. Libre Adj | Free

— *Tu es **libre** de choisir tes études* • You are free to choose your studies

LIBRAIRE

1. Un libraire nm | A bookseller
2. Une libraire nf | A bookseller
3. Une librairie nf | A bookstore

— *La **librairie** est fermée le dimanche* • The bookstore is closed on Sundays

LIER
1. Lier v | To link
2. Un lien nm | A link
3. Une liaison nf | A link
— *Ses symptômes sont **liés** au stress* • His symptoms are linked to stress

LIMITE
1. Une limite nf | A limit
2. Limiter v | To limit
3. Une limitation nf | A limitation
4. Une édition limitée nf | A limited-edition
5. Limité - Limitée Adj | Limited
6. Illimité - Illimitée Adj | Unlimited
— *Une **édition limitée** coute généralement plus cher* • A limited-edition costs usually more

LIT
1. Le lit nm | The bed
2. La literie nf | The bedsheets
— *Notre nouveau **lit** doit être livré dans une semaine* • Our new bed should be delivered in a week

LIVRE
1. Une livre nf | A pound
2. Livrer v | To deliver
3. Un livreur nm | A deliverer
4. Une livreuse nf | A deliverer
5. Une livraison nf | A delivery
— *Le colis pèse deux **livres*** • The package weights two pounds

LOIN
1. Loin Adj | Far

2. Lointain - Lointaine Adj | Distant

— *On peut voir la montagne au **loin*** • We can see the mountain from far away

LONG

1. Long - Longue Adj | Long
2. Longuement Adv | Long
3. Longtemps Adv | Long time
4. La longueur nf | The length

— *Ça fait **longtemps** !* • Long time no see!

LOURD

1. Lourd - Lourde Adj | Heavy
2. Lourdement Adv | Heavily

— *Cette boite est **lourde**, fais attention* • This box is heavy, be careful

LUMIÈRE

1. La lumière nf | The light
2. Lumineux - Lumineuse Adj | Luminous
3. Illuminer v | To illuminate
4. Un luminaire nm | A light
5. La luminosité nf | The brightness

— *C'est une journée **lumineuse** aujourd'hui* • It's a luminous day today

LUNE

1. La lune nf | The moon
2. Lunaire Adj | Lunar

— *On peut admirer la **lune** avec un téléscope* • We can admire the moon with a telescope

Mm.

MAIGRE

1. Maigre Adj | Skinny / Thin
2. La maigreur nf | The thinness
3. Maigrir v | To lose weight
4. Maigrichon - Maigrichonne Adj | Skinny

— *Maigrir trop vite n'est pas bon pour la santé* • Losing weight too fast is not good for your health

MAÎTRISE

1. La maîtrise nf | The control
2. Maîtriser v | To control

— *La maîtrise de ses émotions est importante au travail* • Controlling your emotions is important at work

MALADE

1. Malade Adj | Sick
2. Un malade nm | A sick person
3. Une malade nf | A sick person
4. Une maladie nf | A disease

— *Il ne viendra pas aujourd'hui car il est malade* • He won't come today because he is sick

MANQUE

1. Un manque nm | A lack
2. Manquer v | To miss
3. Un manquement nm | A failure
4. Manquant - Manquante Adj | Lacking

— *Elle me manque beaucoup* • I miss her a lot

MAQUILLER

1. Maquiller v | To disguise
2. Se maquiller v | To apply make-up
3. Le maquillage nm | The make-up
4. Un maquilleur nm | A make-up artist

5. Une maquilleuse nf | A make-up artist

— *Cette **maquilleuse** travaille avec les stars* • This make-up artist works with celebrities

MARCHE

1. Une marche nf | A step
2. Une marche nf | A walk
3. Marcher v | To walk
4. Un marché nm | A market
5. Un marcheur nm | A walker
6. Une marcheuse nf | A walker

— *Attention à la **marche** !* • Watch out for the step!

MARI

1. Un mari nm | A husband
2. Le marié nm | The groom
3. La mariée nf | The bride
4. Se Marier v | To get married
5. Le mariage nm | The marriage / The wedding

— *Nous sommes **mariés** depuis 2 ans* • We have been married for 2 years

MARQUE

1. Une marque nf | A brand
2. Une marque nf | A mark
3. Marquer v | To mark
4. Un marquage nm | A marking
5. Marquant - Marquante Adj | Significant

— *Cette **marque** utilise du coton biologique* • This brand uses organic cotton

MATIN

1. Le matin nm | The morning
2. La matinée nf | The morning
3. Matinal - Matinale Adj | Morning

— *Je suis **matinal**, je me lève tous les jours à 6 heures* • I am a morning person, I get up every day at 6 am

MATURE

1. Mature Adj | Mature
2. La maturité nf | The maturity
3. La maturation nf | The maturation

— *Il est très **mature** pour son âge* • He is very mature for his age

MÉCANIQUE

1. La mécanique nf | The mechanic
2. Mécanique Adj | Mechanical
3. Un mécanicien nm | A mechanic
4. Une mécanicienne nf | A mechanic

— *Mon cousin est passionné de **mécanique*** • My cousin is passionate about mechanics

MÉDECIN

1. Un médecin nm | A doctor
2. La médecine nf | The medicine
3. Médicinal - Médicinale Adj | Medicinal

— *Le **médecin** n'est pas disponible aujourd'hui* • The doctor is not available today

MENACE

1. Une menace nf | A menace / A threat
2. Menacer v | To threat
3. Menaçant - Menaçante Adj | Threating

— *Les koalas sont **menacés** d'extinction* • Koalas are threatened with extinction

MENUISIER

1. Un menuisier nm | A carpenter
2. La menuiserie nf | The carpentry
3. Une menuiserie nf | A carpentry shop

— *Il aimerait devenir **menuisier*** • He would like to become a carpenter

MÉRITE

1. Le mérite nm | The merit
2. Mériter v | To deserve

— *Il a eu de mauvaises notes, il ne **mérite** pas son cadeau* • He got bad grades, he doesn't deserve his gift

MESSAGE

1. Un message nm | A message
2. Un messager nm | A messenger
3. Une messagère nf | A messenger

— *J'ai reçu un **message** d'un numéro inconnu* • I got a message from an unknown number

MEUBLE

1. Un meuble nm | A piece of furniture
2. Meubler v | To furnish
3. L'ameublement nm | The furniture
4. Un garde-meuble nm | A storage facility

— *Nous avons placé toutes nos affaires dans un **garde-meuble*** • We placed all of our belongings in a storage facility

MINCE

1. Mince Adj | Slim
2. La minceur nf | The slimness

— *Elle veut être plus **mince** pour l'été* • She wants to be slimmer for summer

MINUTE

1. Une minute nf | A minute
2. Minuter v | To time
3. Un minuteur nm | A timer
4. Une minuterie nf | A timer
5. Une cocotte-minute nf | A cooker

6. En dernière minute | Last minute

— *Mets la **minuterie** pour 10 minutes s'il te plaît* • Put the timer for 10 minutes please

MIRACLE

1. Un miracle nm | A miracle
2. Miraculeux - Miraculeuse Adj | Miraculous

— *Sa rémission est **miraculeuse** !* • Her remission is miraculous!

MODERNE

1. Moderne Adj | Modern
2. Moderniser v | To modernize
3. La modernisation nf | The modernization

— *Cet appartement est minimaliste et **moderne*** • This apartment is minimalist and modern

MODESTE

1. Modeste Adj | Modest
2. La modestie nf | The modesty
3. Modestement Adv | Modestly

— *Nous avons un **modeste** logement* • We have a modest accommodation

MOMENT

1. Un moment nm | A moment / An instant
2. Momentané - Momentanée Adj | Momentary
3. Momentanément Adv | Momentarily

— *Prends un **moment** pour te relaxer durant la journée* • Take a moment to relax during the day

MONTAGNE

1. La montagne nf | The mountain
2. Montagneux - Montagneuse Adj | Mountainous
3. Un mont nm | A mountain
4. Un montagnard nm | A mountain dweller

5. Une montagnarde nf | A mountain dweller

6. Une montagne russe nf | A roller coaster

— *Nous passons les fêtes de Noël à la **montagne*** • We spend the holidays at the mountain

MONUMENT

1. Un monument nf | A monument

2. Monumental - Monumentale Adj | Monumental

— *Le nouveau **monument** a été inauguré hier* • The new monument was inaugurated yesterday

MORAL

1. Le moral nm | The mood

2. La morale nf | The moral

3. Moralement Adv | Morally

— *La **morale** de l'histoire est de ne pas parler sur le dos des autres* • The moral of the story is that we should not gossip

MORDRE

1. Mordre v | To bite

2. Une morsure nf | A bite

— *La **morsure** peut s'infecter rapidement* • The bite can get infected rapidly

MORT

1. La mort nf | The death

2. Un mort nm | A dead person

3. Une morte nf | A dead person

4. Mortel - Mortelle Adj | Deadly

— *La **mort** de son grand-père a été difficile pour lui* • The death of his grandfather was difficult for him

MOTIVER

1. Motiver v | To motivate

2. La motivation nf | The motivation

114

3. Motivant - Motivante Adj | Motivating

4. Une lettre de motivation nf | A cover letter

— La **motivation** *est importante pour réussir un projet* • Motivation is important to succeed in a project

MOUSTIQUE

1. Un moustique nm | A mosquito

2. Une moustiquaire nf | A mosquito net

— Les **moustiques** *sont problématiques dans beaucoup de pays* • Mosquitoes are problematic in a lot of countries

MOYEN

1. Moyen - Moyenne Adj | Middle

2. Une moyenne nf | An average

3. Le Moyen-Âge nm | The Middle Age

4. Le Moyen-Orient nm | The Middle East

— La **moyenne** *des ventes est positive* • The average of sales is positive

MULTIPLE

1. Multiple Adj | Multiple

2. Un multiple nm | A multiple

3. Multiplier v | To multiply

4. Une multiplication nf | A multiplication

— Ils apprennent les **multiplications** *à l'école* • They learn multiplication at school

MUSCLE

1. Un muscle nm | A muscle

2. La musculature nf | The musculature

3. La musculation nf | The bodybuilding

— Il fait de la **musculation** *3 fois par semaine* • He does bodybuilding 3 times a week

MUSIQUE

1. La musique nf | The music

2. Musical - Musicale Adj | Musical

3. Un musicien nm | A musician

4. Une musicienne nf | A musician

— *Être* **musicien** *demande beaucoup de pratique* • Being a musician takes a lot of practice

Nn.

NAGE

1. La nage nf | The swim
2. Nager v | To swim
3. Un nageur nm | A swimmer
4. Une nageuse nf | A swimmer
5. Un maître-nageur nm | A lifeguard
6. Une maître-nageuse nf | A lifeguard
7. Une nageoire nf | A fin

— *Le **maître-nageur** sera là à 10 heures* • The lifeguard will be there at 10 am

NATURE

1. La nature nf | Nature
2. Naturel - Naturelle Adj | Natural
3. Naturellement Adv | Naturally

— *Rien de meilleur qu'une balade dans la **nature*** • Nothing is better than a walk in nature

NAVIGUER

1. Naviguer v | To navigate
2. La navigation nf | The navigation
3. Un navigateur nm | A navigator
4. Une navigatrice nf | A navigator

— *Christophe Colomb était un **navigateur*** • Christophe Colomb was a navigator

NÉCESSAIRE

1. Nécessaire Adj | Necessary
2. Le nécessaire nm | The essentials
3. Nécessairement Adv | Necessarily
4. Une nécessité nf | A need

— *Ce n'est pas **nécessairement** vrai* • It's not necessarily true

NÉGOCIER

1. Négocier v | To negotiate

2. Une négociation nf | A negotiation

3. Négociable Adj | Negotiable

4. Un négociant nm | A dealer

5. Une négociante nf | A dealer

—— *Il **négocie** le prix de la voiture avec le vendeur* • He is negotiating the price of the car with the salesman

NEIGE

1. La neige nf | The snow

2. Neiger v | To snow

3. Neigeux - Neigeuse Adj | Snowy

4. Une motoneige nf | A snowmobile

5. Un chasse-neige nm | A snow plow

—— *Avoir de la **neige** pour Noël est magique* • Having snow for Christmas is magical

NERVEUX

1. Nerveux - Nerveuse Adj | Nervous

2. Nerveusement Adv | Nervously

3. Un nerf nm | A nerve

4. Énerver v | To anger

—— *Il est **nerveux** à cause de ses examens* • He is nervous because of his exams

NOISETTE

1. Une noisette nf | A hazelnut

2. Un noisetier nm | A hazel tree

3. Un casse-noisettes nm | A nutcracker

—— *Les **noisettes** sont populaires dans les recettes automnales* • Hazelnuts are popular in autumn recipes

NOM

1. Un nom nm | A name

2. Nommer v | To appoint

3. Un nom de famille nm | A surname

4. Un prénom nm | A first name

— *Elle gardera son **nom de famille** après le mariage* • She will keep her surname after the wedding

NOMINER

1. Nominer v | To nominate
2. Une nomination nf | A nomination
3. Un nominé nm | A nominee
4. Une nominée nf | A nominee

— *Cet artiste est **nominé** pour les Oscars* • This artist is nominated for the Oscars

NORD

1. Le nord nm | The north
2. Nordique Adj | Nordic
3. Le Pôle Nord nm | The North Pole

— *Le Père Noël habite au **Pôle Nord*** • Santa lives in the North Pole

NORMAL

1. Normal - Normale Adj | Normal
2. Normaliser v | To normalize
3. La normalisation nf | The normalisation
4. Normalement Adv | Normally

— *Le colis devrait arriver aujourd'hui **normalement*** • Normally the package should arrive today

NOTE

1. Une note nf | A note
2. Noter v | To note
3. Un notebook nm | A notebook

— *J'ai besoin d'un nouveau **notebook*** • I need a new notebook

NOURRIR

1. Nourrir v | To feed
2. La nourriture nf | The food

3. Nourrissant - Nourrissante Adj | Nourishing

4. Une nourrice nf | A nanny

5. Un nourrisson nm | An infant

— *Mon fils est avec sa **nourrice*** • My son is with his nanny

NOUVEAU

1. Nouveau - Nouvel - Nouvelle Adj | New

2. Une nouveauté nf | A novelty

3. Renouveler v | To renew

4. Un renouvellement nm | A renewal

5. Renouvelable Adj | Renewable

— *Le **renouvellement** de l'abonnement est en janvier de l'année prochaine*
• The renewal of the subscription is in January next year

NUAGE

1. Un nuage nm | A cloud

2. Nuageux - Nuageuse Adj | Cloudy

— *Le ciel est **nuageux** aujourd'hui* • This sky is cloudy today

NUTRITION

1. La nutrition nf | The nutrition

2. Un nutritionniste nm | A nutritionist

3. Une nutritionniste nf | A nutritionist

4. Nutritif - Nutritive Adj | Nutritious

5. Nutritionnel - Nutritionnelle Adj | Nutritional

— *Un **nutritionniste** travaille avec des personnes de tout âge* •
A nutritionist works with people of all ages

OBÉIR

1. Obéir v | To obey
2. Obéissant - Obéissante Adj | Obedient
3. L'obéissance nf | The obedience
— *Ce chiot n'est pas* **obéissant** • This puppy is not obedient

OBÈSE

1. Obèse Adj | Obese
2. L'obésité nf | The obesity
— *L'***obésité** *est un problème de santé majeur* • Obesity is a major health problem

OBJET

1. Un objet nm | An object
2. Objectif - Objective Adj | Objective
3. Un objectif nm | An objective
— *Qu'est-ce que cet* **objet** *?* • What is this object?

OBLIGER

1. Obliger v | To force
2. Une obligation nf | An obligation
3. Obligatoire Adj | Mandatory
— *Voter devrait être* **obligatoire** • Voting should be mandatory

OBSERVER

1. Observer v | To observe
2. Une observation nf | An observation
3. Un observatoire nm | An observatory
4. Un observateur nm | An observer
5. Une observatrice nf | An observer
— *On peut admirer les étoiles à l'***observatoire** • We can admire the stars at the observatory

OBTENIR

1. Obtenir v | To obtain
2. Une obtention nf | An acquisition
3. Obtenu - Obtenue Adj | Obtained

— *J'ai **obtenu** les informations dont j'avais besoin* • I obtained the information I needed

OCCASION

1. Une occasion nf | An occasion
2. Occasionnel - Occasionnelle Adj | Occasional
3. Occasionnellement Adv | Occasionally
4. Occasioner v | To cause

— *C'est une parfaite **occasion** pour rencontrer tes collègues* • This is a perfect occasion to meet your colleagues

OCCUPER

1. Occuper v | To occupy
2. Une occupation nf | An occupation
3. Un occupant nm | An occupant
4. Une occupante nf | An occupant

— *Ils **occupent** les bureaux depuis 2 ans* • They've been occupying the offices for the past 2 years

OFFRIR

1. Offrir v | To offer
2. Une offre nf | An offer
3. Une offre de prix nf | A price offer

— *Que vas-tu **offrir** pour le mariage ?* • What are you going to offer for the wedding?

OLIVE

1. Une olive nf | An olive
2. Un olivier nm | An olive tree
3. De l'huile d'olive nf | Olive oil

— *Je préfère acheter des* **olives** *sans noyaux* • I prefer to buy olives without pits

OPÉRATION

1. Une opération nf | An operation / A surgery
2. Opérer v | To operate
3. Opérationnel - Opérationnelle Adj | Operational
4. Un opérateur nm | An operator
5. Une opératrice nf | An operator
6. Un bloc opératoire nm | An operating room

— *L'***opératrice** *téléphonique tente d'aider les clients* • The phone operator tries to help customers

OPPOSER

1. Opposer v | To oppose
2. Un opposé nm | An opposite
3. Une opposée nf | An opposite
4. Une opposition v | An opposition
5. Opposable Adj | Opposable

— *Les habitants s'***opposent** *à la construction de la nouvelle usine* • The residents oppose the construction of the new factory

OPTIMISER

1. Optimiser v | To optimize
2. Optimiste Adj | Optimistic
3. L'optimisme nm | The optimism
4. L'optimisation nf | The optimisation

— *L'***optimisation** *du programme était plus que nécessaire* • The software optimisation was more than necessary

OPTION

1. Une option nf | An option
2. Optionnel - Optionnelle Adj | Optional

— *Les sièges chauffants sont* **optionnels** • The heated seats are optional

127

OREILLE

1. Une oreille nf | An ear
2. Un oreiller nm | A pillow
3. Une oreillette nf | A headset
4. Les oreillons nm | The mumps
5. Une taie d'oreiller nf | A pillowcase
6. Un cache-oreilles nm | Earmuffs
7. Une boucle d'oreille nf | An earring

—— *Elle s'est fait percer les **oreilles** en vacances* • She got her ears pierced on vacation

ORGANISER

1. Organiser v | To organize
2. Une organisation nf | An organisation
3. Un organisateur nm | An organizer
4. Une organisatrice nf | An organizer

—— *L'**organisation** de cet évènement était parfaite* • The organisation of this event was perfect

ORIENTER

1. Orienter v | To direct
2. Une orientation nf | An orientation
3. Désorienter v | To disorient
4. La désorientation nf | The disorientation
5. Désorienté - Désorientée Adj | Disoriented

—— *La déshydratation peut causer la **désorientation*** • Dehydration can cause disorientation

OS

1. Un os nm | A bone
2. Une ossature nf | A backbone
3. Un ossement nm | A bone
4. La moelle osseuse nf | The bone marrow

—— *Le chien a enterré son **os** dans le jardin* • The dog buried his bone in the backyard

OUBLI

1. Un oubli nm | An oblivion
2. Oublier v | To forget
3. Les oubliettes nf | The dungeons

— *Il **oublie** toujours tout* • He always forgets everything

OURS

1. Un ours nm | A bear
2. Un ourson nm | A cub
3. Un ours en peluche nm | A teddy bear

— *Le bébé a perdu son **ours en peluche*** • The baby lost her teddy bear

OUTIL

1. Un outil nm | A tool
2. Un outillage nm | A set of tools
3. Une boîte à outils nf | A toolbox

— *Peux-tu aller chercher ma **boîte à outils** dans le garage s'il te plaît ?* • Can you go get my toolbox from the garage please?

OUVERT

1. Ouvert - Ouverte Adj | Open
2. Une ouverture nf | An opening
3. Ouvrir v | To open

— *Le magasin est **ouvert** à partir de 10 heures* • The shop is open from 10am

Pp.

PÂLE

1. Pâle Adj | Pale
2. La pâleur nf | The paleness
3. Pâlir v | To fade

— *Ce rouge **pâle** ira très bien dans le salon* • This pale red will be perfect in the living room

PARADIS

1. Le paradis nm | The paradise / Heaven
2. Paradisiaque Adj | Heavenly / Paradisiacal

— *J'aimerais passer une semaine sur une île **paradisiaque*** • I would like to spend a week on a paradisiacal island

PARESSE

1. La paresse nf | The laziness
2. Paresseux - Paresseuse Adj | Lazy
3. Paresser v | To lounge
4. Paresseusement Adv | Lazily

— *La **paresse** empêche de réaliser ses rêves* • Laziness stops you from realizing your dreams

PARFUM

1. Un parfum nm | A perfume
2. Parfumer v | To perfume
3. Une parfumerie nf | A perfumery
4. Un parfumeur nm | A perfumer

— *On peut créer son **parfum** soi-même à Paris* • We can create perfume ourselves in Paris

PARLER

1. Parler v | To speak
2. La parole nf | The speaking

— *Il **parle** 4 langues* • He speaks 4 languages

PARTICIPER

1. Participer v | To participate
2. Un participant nm | A participant
3. Une participante nf | A participant
4. La participation nf | The participation
5. Participant - Participante Adj | Participating

— *Il n'est pas nécessaire d'acheter le* ***produit*** *pour participer au concours* • It's not necessary to buy the product to participate in the contest

PARTICULIER

1. Particulier - Particulière Adj | Particular
2. Particulièrement Adv | Particularly
3. Une particularité nf | A particularity

— *J'aime beaucoup ce pullover,* ***particulièrement*** *le bleu* • I really like this sweater, particularly in blue

PASSION

1. Une passion nf | A passion
2. Passionner v | To fascinate
3. Passionné - Passionnée Adj | Passionate
4. Passionnément Adv | Passionately
5. Passionnant - Passionnante Adj | Exciting
6. Un fruit de la passion nm | A passion fruit

— *Il aime sa fiancée* ***passionnément*** • He loves his fiancée passionately

PATIENTER

1. Patienter v | To wait
2. Un patient nm | A patient
3. Une patiente nf | A patient
4. Patient - Patiente Adj | Patient
5. La patience nf | The patience
6. Impatient - Impatiente Adj | Impatient
7. L'impatiente nf | The impatience
8. Patiemment Adv | Patiently
9. Impatiemment Adv | Impatiently

— *Tu devras être **patient** pour recevoir tes cadeaux* • You will have to be patient to get your gifts

PÂTISSERIE

1. Une pâtisserie nf | A pastry
2. Une pâtisserie nf | A bakery
3. Un pâtissier nm | A pastry cook
4. Une pâtissière nf | A pastry cook
5. Une crème pâtissière nf | A pastry cream
6. Un rouleau à pâtisserie nm | A rolling pin

— *Ma **pâtisserie** préférée est le mille-feuilles* • My favourite pastry is a mille-feuilles

PAUVRE

1. Pauvre Adj | Poor
2. Un pauvre nm | A poor man
3. Une pauvre nf | A poor woman
4. La pauvreté nf | The poverty

— *La **pauvreté** devient de plus en plus fréquente* • Poverty is becoming more and more frequent

PEINTURE

1. Une peinture nf | A painting
2. De la peinture nf | Some paint
3. Un peintre nm | A painter
4. Une peintre nf | A painter
5. Peindre v | To paint
6. Le papier peint nm | The wallpaper

— *Nous allons enlever le **papier peint** et peindre la pièce* • We will remove the wallpaper and paint the room

PENSER

1. Penser v | To think
2. Une pensée nf | A thought
3. Un penseur nm | A thinker

4. Une penseuse nf | A thinker

5. Pensif - Pensive Adj | Thoughtful

6. Un pense-bête nm | A reminder

— *Je **penserai** à vous durant mon voyage* • I will think about you during my journey

PENSION

1. Une pension nf | A pension

2. Un pensionné nm | A retired man / pensioner

3. Une pensionnée nf | A retired woman / pensioner

4. Pensionner v | To retire

5. Un pensionnat nm | A residential school

6. Un pensionnaire nm | A resident

7. Une pensionnaire nf | A resident

— *Mes parents sont **pensionnés** depuis l'année dernière* • My parents have been retired since last year

PERDRE

1. Perdre v | To lose

2. Perdu - Perdue Adj | Lost

3. Un perdant nm | A loser

4. Une perdante nf | A loser

5. La perte nf | The loss

— *Je **perds** toujours aux cartes* • I always lose at cards

PERMIS

1. Un permis nm | A license

2. Un permis de conduire nm | A driving license

3. Une permission nf | A permission

4. Permettre v | To allow

5. Permis - Permise Adj | Allowed

— *Mon frère a réussi son **permis de conduire*** • My brother got his driving license

PERSONNE

1. Une personne nf | A person
2. Du personnel nm | Staff
3. Personnel - Personnelle Adj | Personal
4. Une personnalité nf | A personality
5. Personnellement Adv | Personally

— *Nous sommes en manque de **personnel*** • We are in need of more staff

PERSUADER

1. Persuader v | To persuade
2. La persuasion nf | The persuasion
3. Persuasif - Persuasive Adj | Persuasive

— *Il est **persuadé** que sa femme a une relation* • He was persuaded that his wife has an affair

PESSIMISME

1. Le pessimisme nm | The pessimism
2. Pessimiste Adj | Pessimistic
3. Un pessimiste nm | A pessimist
4. Une pessimiste nf | A pessimist

— *Il est toujours **pessimiste** quand il s'agit de ses projets* • He is always pessimistic when it comes to his projects

PEUR

1. La peur nf | The fear
2. Peureux - Peureuse Adj | Fearful
3. Peureusement Adv | Fearfully
4. Apeurer v | To scare

— *Notre chat était **peureux** quand nous l'avons adopté* • Our cat was fearful when we adopted him

PHARMACIE

1. Une pharmacie nf | A pharmacy
2. Un pharmacien nm | A pharmacist

3. Une pharmacienne nf | A pharmacist

4. Pharmaceutique Adj | Pharmaceutical

5. Une armoire à pharmacie nf | A medicine cabinet

— *Regarde dans l'**armoire à pharmacie** s'il y a des pansements* •
Look in the medicine cabinet to see if there are bandage

PHILOSOPHE

1. Un philosophe nm | A philosopher

2. Une philosophe nf | A philosopher

3. La philosophie nf | The philosophy

4. Philosophique Adj | Philosophical

— *La **philosophie** est un sujet abstrait* • Philosophy is an abstract
subject

PHOTO

1. Une photo nf | A photo

2. Une photographie nf | A photograph

3. La photographie nf | The photography

4. Photographier v | To photograph

5. Un photographe nm | A photographer

6. Une photographe nf | A photographer

7. Photogénique Adj | Photogenic

8. Un appareil photo nm | A camera

9. Une séance de photos nf | A photo shoot

— *Prenons une **photo** devant ce monument* • Let's take a picture in front
of this monument

PIANO

1. Un piano nm | A piano

2. Un pianiste nm | A pianist

3. Une pianiste nf | A pianist

— *C'est mieux d'apprendre le **piano** quand on est petit* • It's better to
learn piano when you are young

PLACER

1. Placer v | To place
2. Une place nf | A place
3. Une place nf | A square
4. Un placement nm | A placement
5. Une mise en place nf | An implementation

— *Peux-tu nous garder deux **places** près de toi ?* • Can you save two places close to you?

PLAFOND

1. Un plafond nm | A ceiling
2. Un plafonnier nm | A ceiling light
3. Plafonner v | To cap

— *Le **plafond** doit être repeint* • The ceiling needs to be repainted

PLAISIR

1. Le plaisir nm | The pleasure
2. Plaisant - Plaisante Adj | Pleasant

— *Je fais du sport juste pour le **plaisir*** • I play sport just for pleasure

PLAN

1. Un plan nm | A plan
2. Planifier v | To plan
3. La planification nf | The planning
4. Un planificateur nm | A planner
5. Une planificatrice nf | A planner

— *Quel est le **plan** pour les vacances?* • What's the plan for the vacation?

PLANTE

1. Une plante nf | A plant
2. Planter v | To plant
3. Une plantation nf | A plantation

— *S'occuper des **plantes** est comme une thérapie pour moi* • Taking care of the plants is like therapy for me

PLAT

1. Un plat nm | A dish
2. Un plateau nm | A tray
3. Plat - Plate Adj | Flat

— *Il y a des toasts sur le **plateau*** • There is toast on the tray

PLIER

1. Plier v | To fold
2. Un pliage nm | A folding
3. Pliable Adj | Foldable

— ***Pliez** la feuille de papier comme indiqué* • Fold the piece of paper as indicated

POCHE

1. Une poche nf | A pocket
2. Une pochette nf | A pouch
3. Empocher v | To pocket
4. L'argent de poche nm | The pocket money
5. Une lampe de poche nf | A flashlight

— *Peux-tu mettre mes clés dans ta **poche** ?* • Can you put my keys in your pocket?

POÈTE

1. Un poète nm | A poet
2. Une poète nf | A poet
3. Un poème nm | A poem
4. La poésie nf | The poetry

— *Il vient de publier un livre de **poésie*** • He just published a poetry book

POINT

1. Un point nm | A point
2. Le pointage nm | The score
3. Pointer v | To point
4. Pointilleux - Pointilleuse Adj | Picky
5. Pointillé - Pointillée Adj | Dotted

— *Elle est très **pointilleuse** dans ses dessins* •She is very picky with her drawings

POIRE
1. Une poire nf | A pear
2. Un poirier nm | A pear tree
   — *Les **poires** sont mûres* • The pears are ripe

POIVRE
1. Le poivre nm | The pepper
2. Une poivrière nf | A pepper shaker
3. Poivrer v | To pepper
   — *La cuisinière **poivre** le steak* • The chef is peppering the steak

POLI
1. Poli - Polie Adj | Polite
2. La politesse nf | The politeness
3. Poliment Adv | Politely
   — *Elle demande **poliment** sa direction* •She asks politely for direction

POLITIQUE
1. La politique nf | The politics
2. Politiquement Adv | Politically
3. Politique Adj | Political
4. Un politicien nm | A politician
5. Une politicienne nf | A politician
   — *Le **politicien** voyage beaucoup pour son travail* • The politician travels a lot for his work

POLLUER
1. Polluer v | To pollute
2. La pollution nf | The pollution
3. Un polluant nm | A pollutant
4. Polluant - Polluante Adj | Polluting

— La **pollution** *devrait être au cœur des problèmes à résoudre* •
Pollution should be the main problem to resolve

POMME

1. Une pomme nf | An apple
2. Un pommier nm | An apple tree
3. Une pomme de terre nf | A potato
4. La compote de pommes nf | The applesauce

— *Je prépare de la* **compote de pommes** *pour ce soir* • I am
making applesauce for tonight

POMPER

1. Pomper v | To pump
2. Une pompe nf | A pump
3. Un pompier nm | A firefighter
4. Un camion de pompier nm | A fire truck
5. Une caserne de pompier nf | A fire station

— La **pompe** *de la chaudière doit être remplacée* • The pump of
the furnace must be replaced

PORTE

1. La porte nf | The door
2. Une portière nf | A car door
3. Un portier nm | A porter

— *Laisse les clés au* **portier** *avant de partir* • Leave the key to the
porter before leaving

PORTER

1. Porter v | To carry
2. Un porteur nm | A porter
3. Une porteuse nf | A porter
4. Portant - Portante Adj | Supporting

— *Mon père ne peut plus rien* **porter** *de lourd à cause de son dos* •
My father can't carry anything heavy anymore because of his back

POSSIBLE

1. Possible Adj | Possible
2. Une possibilité nf | A possibility

— *Changer de travail est une **possibilité*** • Changing jobs is a possibility

POTENTIEL

1. Potentiel - Potentielle Adj | Potential
2. Potentiellement Adv | Potentially

— *Il y aurait à priori un acheteur **potentiel*** • At first there would be a potential buyer

POUDRE

1. La poudre nf | The powder
2. Poudreux - Poudreuse Adj | Powdery

— *La neige est **poudreuse** cette année* • The snow is powdery this year

POURCENT

1. Un pourcent nm | A percent
2. Un pourcentage nm | A percentage

— *Le vendeur reçoit un **pourcentage** des ventes* • The salesman gets a percentage of the sales

POUVOIR

1. Pouvoir v | May / Can
2. Le pouvoir nm | The power

— *Mon frère devrait **pouvoir** rentrer pour Noël* • My brother may be able to come home for Christmas

PRATIQUE

1. Une pratique nf | A practice
2. Pratique Adj | Practical
3. Pratiquer v | To practice
4. Pratiquant - Pratiquante Adj | Practising
5. Pratiquement Adv | Practically

— ***Pratiquer*** *un sport est important pour la santé* • Practising a sport is important for your health

PRÉCÉDER

1. Précéder v | To precede
2. Un précédent nm | A precedent
3. Une précédente nf | A precedent
4. Précédent - Précédente Adj | Previous
5. Précédemment Adv | Previously

— *Ce qui s'est passé* ***précédemment*** *n'a pas d'importance* • What happened previously is not important

PRÉDIRE

1. Prédire v | To predict
2. Une prédiction nf | A prediction

— *Il va neiger selon les* ***prédictions*** *météorologiques* • It's going to snow according to the weather prediction

PRÉFÉRER

1. Préférer v | To prefer
2. Préféré - Préférée Adj | Preferred
3. Une préférence nf | A preference
4. Préférable Adj | Preferable

— *J'ai une* ***préférence*** *pour la robe bleue* • I have a preference for the blue dress

PRÉPARER

1. Préparer v | To prepare
2. Une préparation nf | A preparation
3. Un préparatif nm | A preparation
4. Préparatoire Adj | Preparatory

— *Une bonne* ***préparation*** *est essentielle pour réussir* • Proper preparation is essential to succeed.

PRÉCISER

1. Préciser v | To specify
2. Précis - Précise Adj | Specific
3. La précision nf | The precision
4. Précisément Adv | Precisely

— *Ils se sont perdus malgré la **précision** de la carte* • They got lost despite the precision of the map

PRESCRIRE

1. Prescrire v | To prescribe
2. Une prescription nf | A prescription
3. Prescrit - Prescrite Adj | Prescribed

— *Sa **prescription** doit être renouvelée tous les 2 mois* • His prescription must be renewed every 2 months

PRÉSENTER

1. Présenter v | To present
2. Une présentation nf | A presentation
3. Une présence nf | A presence
4. Présent - Présente Adj | Present

— *La **présentation** a convaincu le jury* • The presentation convinced the jury

PRÉSERVER

1. Préserver v | To preserve
2. La préservation nf | The preservation
3. Un préservateur nm | A preservative
4. Un préservatif nm | A condom

— *La **préservation** des monuments historiques est essentielle pour l'Histoire* • Preservation of historical monuments is essential for the History

PRÉSIDER

1. Présider v | To preside
2. Un président nm | A president
3. Une présidente nf | A president

4. La présidence nf | The presidency

5. Présidentiel - Présidentielle Adj | Presidential

—— *Le **président** arrivera demain à Paris par avion* • The president will arrive tomorrow in Paris by plane

PRINCE

1. Un prince nm | A prince

2. Une princesse nf | A princess

3. Princier - Princière Adj | Royal

—— *Les enfants aiment se déguiser en **princesse*** • Children like to dress up as princesses

PRISON

1. Une prison nf | A prison

2. Un prisonnier nm | A prisoner

3. Une prisonnière nf | A prisoner

4. Emprisonner v | To imprison

5. Un emprisonnement nm | An imprisonment

—— *Les gardiens de la **prison** commencent une grève demain* • Prison guards start a strike tomorrow

PROBABLE

1. Probable Adj | Likely

2. Probablement Adv | Probably

3. Une probabilité nf | A probability

—— *Il y aura **probablement** d'autres opportunités* • There will probably be other opportunities

PROBLÈME

1. Un problème nm | A problem

2. Problématique Adj | Problematic

—— *La maîtresse explique le **problème** de mathématique* • The teacher explains the math problem

PROCHAIN

1. Prochain - Prochaine Adj | Next

2. Prochainement Adv | Soon

— *Elles doivent acheter leurs billets d'avion **prochainement*** • They have to buy their plane tickets soon

PRODUIRE

1. Produire v | To produce

2. Un produit nm | A product

3. Une production nf | A production

— *La **production** de l'usine est limitée durant le week-end* • The factory's production is limited during the weekend

PROFESSION

1. Une profession nf | A profession

2. Un professionnel nm | A professional

3. Une professionnelle nf | A professional

4. Professionnel - Professionnelle Adj | Professional

— *Il n'a pas encore fini ses études mais se considère déjà comme un **professionnel*** • He isn't done with his studies yet but he already considers himself a professional

PROFOND

1. Profond - Profonde Adj | Deep

2. La profondeur nf | The depth

3. Profondément Adv | Deeply

— *Ce lac est un des plus **profond*** • This lake is one of the deepest

PROGRAMME

1. Un programme nm | A program

2. Programmer v | To program

3. Un programmeur nm | A programmer

4. Une programmatrice nf | A programmer

— *Le **programme** du spectacle est distribué à l'entrée* • The spectacle's program is distributed at the entrance

145

PROGRESSER

1. Progresser v | To progress
2. Une progression nf | A progression
3. Un progrès nm | A progress
4. Progressif - Progressive Adj | Progressive

—— *Ma tante fait beaucoup de **progrès** dans son régime* • My aunt is making a lot of progress on her diet

PROJET

1. Un projet nm | A project
2. Projeter v | To project
3. Un projecteur nm | A projector

—— *Le projet sera **présenté** bientôt à l'administration* • The project will be presented soon to the administration

PROMENER

1. Promener v | To walk
2. Une promenade nf | A walk
3. Un promeneur nm | A walker
4. Une promeneuse nf | A walker

—— *Un chien a besoin de se **promener** 2 à 3 fois par jour* • A dog needs to walk 2 to 3 times a day

PROPOSER

1. Proposer v | To offer
2. Une proposition nf | A suggestion
3. Un propos nm | A statement

—— *La **proposition** de l'architecte est au-dessus du budget* • The architect's suggestion is over the budget

PROUVER

1. Prouver v | To prove
2. Une preuve nf | A proof
3. Prouvé - Prouvée Adj | Proven

—— *Cela ne **prouve** rien* • This doesn't prove anything

146

PROVISION

1. Une provision nf | A provision
2. Approvisionner v | To supply
3. Un approvisionnement nf | A supply

— *Le magasin est* **approvisionné** *chaque jour* • The store is supplied every day

PRUDENCE

1. La prudence nf | The prudence
2. Prudent - Prudente Adj | Prudent
3. Prudemment Adv | Carefully

— *Nous devons conduire* **prudemment** *sur la neige* • We need to drive carefully in the snow

PRUNE

1. Une prune nf | A plum
2. Un prunier nm | A plum tree

— *Ces* **prunes** *sont parfaitement sucrées* • These plums are perfectly sweet

PSYCHIATRE

1. Un psychiatre nm | A psychiatrist
2. Une psychiatre nf | A psychiatrist
3. Psychiatrique Adj | Psychiatric
4. La psychiatrie nf | The psychiatry

— *Le* **psychiatre** *insiste pour un traitement de longue durée* • The psychiatrist insists on a long-term treatment

PSYCHOLOGUE

1. Un psychologue nm | A psychologist
2. Une psychologue nf | A psychologist
3. La psychologie nf | The psychology
4. Psychologique Adj | Psychological
5. Psychologiquement Adv | Psychologically

— *Le* **psychologue** *ne prescrit pas de médicaments* • The psychologist doesn't prescribe medicine

PUBLIC

1. Le public nm | The public
2. Public - Publique Adj | Public
3. Publiquement Adv | Publicly

— *Le **public** attend le début du concert* • The public is waiting for the beginning of the concert

PUBLIER

1. Publier v | To publish
2. Une publicité nf | An advertisement
3. Une publication nf | A publication

— *Son livre sera **publié** dans 2 semaines* • His book will be published in 2 weeks

Qq.

QUALIFIER
1. Qualifier v | To qualify
2. Une qualification nf | A qualification
3. Qualifié - Qualifiée Adj | Qualified
— *Les **qualifications** ont lieu en juillet* • Qualifications take place in July

QUESTION
1. Une question nf | A question
2. Questionner v | To question
3. Un questionnaire nm | A questionnaire
— *Les élèves ont rempli le **questionnaire*** • Students completed the questionnaire

QUOTIDIEN
1. Le quotidien nm | The quotidian
2. Quotidiennement Adv | Daily
— *Il lit le journal **quotidiennement*** • He reads the newspaper daily

Rr.

RADIEUX

1. Radieux - Radieuse Adj | Bright
2. Une radiation nf | A radiation
3. Un radiateur nm | A radiator

— *Allume le* **radiateur** *s'il te plaît* • Turn on the radiator please

RAISON

1. La raison nf | The reason
2. Raisonner v | To reason
3. Raisonnable Adj | Reasonable
4. Un raisonnement nm | A reasoning
5. En raison de Prép | Due to

— *Il est impossible à* **raisonner** • He is impossible to reason with

RANDONNÉE

1. Une randonnée nf | A hike
2. Un randonneur nm | A hiker
3. Une randonneuse nf | A hiker

— *Cette* **randonnée** *dure 8 heures* • This hike takes 8 hours

RANGER

1. Ranger v | To tidy
2. Un rangement nm | A storage unit / A storage space

— *Nous avons besoin de plus de* **rangements** • We need more storage space

RAPIDE

1. Rapide Adj | Fast
2. Rapidement Adv | Quickly
3. La rapidité nf | The rapidity

— *Les Greyhounds sont des chiens* **rapides** • Greyhounds are fast dogs

RAPPORT

1. Un rapport nm | A report
2. Rapporter v | To report

— *Le **rapport** montre bien les erreurs* • The report shows the mistakes

RASER

1. Raser v | To shave
2. Un rasoir nm | A razor
3. Une lame de rasoir nf | A razor blade
4. Un rasoir électrique nm | An electric shaver
5. Un rasoir jetable nm | A disposable razor

— *Il a reçu un **rasoir électrique** pour Noël* • He got an electric shaver for Christmas

RASSEMBLER

1. Rassembler v | To gather
2. Un rassemblement nm | A gathering

— *Le **rassemblement** aura lieu samedi prochain* • The gathering will take place next Saturday

RAYON

1. Un rayon nm | A ray
2. Rayonner v | To shine
3. Le rayonnement nm | The radiation
4. Rayonnant - Rayonnante Adj | Radiant

— *Enfin un **rayon** de soleil !* • Finally, a ray of sunshine!

RÉACTION

1. Une réaction nf | A reaction
2. La réactivité nf | The reactivity
3. Réactif - Réactive Adj | Reactive
4. Réagir v | To react
5. Réagissant - Réagissante Adj | Reacting

— *Sa **réaction** est parfaitement compréhensible* • Her reaction is perfectly understandable

RÉALISER

1. Réaliser v | To realize

2. La réalisation nf | The achievement / The realisation

3. Réaliste Adj | Realistic

4. Un réalisateur nm | A director

5. Une réalisatrice nf | A director

6. Réalisable Adj | Achievable

— La **réalisation** *de ce projet a pris 2 ans* • The realisation of this project took 2 years

REBELLE

1. Un rebelle nm | A rebel

2. Rebelle Adj | Rebel

3. Rebeller v | To rebel

4. Une rébellion nm | A rebellion

— *Les adolescents se* **rebellent** *contre leurs parents* • Teenagers rebel against their parents

RECEVOIR

1. Recevoir v | To receive

2. Un reçu nm | A receipt

3. Une réception nf | A reception

4. Recevant Adj | Receiving

5. Recevable Adj | Admissible

6. La recevabilité nf | The admissibility

— *Puis-je avoir le* **reçu** *?* • May I have the receipt?

RECOMMANDER

1. Recommander v | To recommend

2. Une recommandation nf | A recommendation

— *Il a été engagé sur* **recommandation** • He got hired on recommendation

RÉCOMPENSE

1. Une récompense nf | A reward

2. Récompenser v | To reward

— *Il sera **récompensé** pour ses efforts* • He will be rewarded for his effort

RÉCUPÉRER

1. Récupérer v | To recover
2. La récupération nf | The recovery
   — *Il a **récupéré** plus vite que prévu* • He recovered faster than expected

RÉDACTION

1. La rédaction nf | The writing
2. Un rédacteur nm | An editor
3. Une rédactrice nf | An editor
4. Rédactionnel - Rédactionnelle Adj | Editorial
   — *Le **rédacteur** est absent aujourd'hui* • The editor is absent today

REFUS

1. Un refus nm | A refusal
2. Refuser v | To refuse
   — *Le docteur **refuse** de performer l'opération* • The doctor refuses to perform the surgery

REGARD

1. Le regard nm | The look
2. Regarder v | To look
   — *Il **regarde** par la fenêtre* • He is looking out the window

RÉGION

1. Une région nm | A region
2. Régional - Régionale Adj | Regional
   — *La Suisse a de très jolies **régions*** • Switzerland has beautiful regions

RÉGULARISER

1. Régulariser v | To regularize
2. La régularisation nf | The regularization

3. La régularité nf | The regularity / The consistency

— *La **régularité** est essentielle pour apprendre quelque chose de nouveau* • Consistency is essential when learning something new

RÉGULIER

1. Régulier - Régulière Adj | Regular
2. Régulièrement Adv | Regularly

— *Mon frère souffre **régulièrement** de migraines* • My brother suffers regularly from migraines

RELAXER

1. Relaxer v | To relax
2. Relaxant - Relaxante Adj | Relaxing
3. Relax Adj | Relaxed
4. La relaxation nf | Relaxation

— *Prendre un bain est **relaxant*** • Talking a bath is relaxing

RELIGION

1. Une religion nf | A religion
2. Religieux - religieuse Adj | Religious
3. Religieusement Adv | Religiously
4. Un religieux nm | A priest
5. Une religieuse nf | A nun

— *Tout le monde a une **religion** différente* • Everybody has a different religion

REMERCIER

1. Remercier v | To thank
2. Un remerciement nm | A gratitude / A thank you
3. Un merci nm | A thank you

— *Les jeunes mariés ont **remerciés** leurs invités* • The newlyweds thanked their guests

RENCONTRER

1. Rencontrer v | To meet

2. Une rencontre nf | A meeting

— *Nous avons eu la chance de le **rencontrer*** • We had the chance to meet him

RÉPARER

1. Réparer v | To repair

2. Une réparation nf | A repair

— *Le mécanicien **répare** les voitures* • The mechanic repairs cars

REPASSER

1. Repasser v | To iron

2. Le repassage nm | The ironing

3. Un fer à repasser nm | An iron

4. Une table à repasser nf | An ironing board

— *Je fais le **repassage** devant la télé* • I do the ironing in front of the TV

RÉPONDRE

1. Répondre v | To answer

2. Une réponse nf | An answer

3. Un répondeur nm | An answering machine

4. Le répondant nm | The respondent

— *Laissez un message sur le **répondeur*** • Leave a message on the answering machine

REPRÉSENTER

1. Représenter v | To represent

2. La représentation nf | The representation

3. Représentatif - Représentative Adj | Representative

4. Un représentant nm | A representative

5. Une représentante nf | A representative

— *Un **représentant** va venir montrer les nouveaux produits* • A representative will come show the new products

REPORTER

1. Reporter v | To postpone

2. Un reporter nm | A reporter

3. Un reportage nm | A documentary

— *Il est le réalisateur d'un **reportage** sur l'environnement* • He is the director of a documentary about the environment

RÉSERVER

1. Réserver v | To book

2. Une réservation nf | A reservation

3. Une réserve nf | A reserve

4. Un réservoir nm | A tank

— *Nous avons une **réservation** pour deux* • We have a reservation for two

RÉSIDER

1. Résider v | To reside

2. Résident - Résidente Adj | Resident

3. Un résident nm | A resident

4. Une résidente nf | A resident

5. Une résidence nf | A residence

— *Notre **résidence** secondaire se trouve en Irlande* • Our secondary residence is in Ireland

RÉSISTER

1. Résister v | To resist

2. Résistant - Résistante Adj | Resistant

3. La résistance nf | The resistance

— *L'ingénieur a été informé du problème de **résistance*** • The engineer has been informed of the resistance problem

RESPECT

1. Le respect nm | The respect

2. Respecter v | To respect

3. Respectable Adj | Respectable

4. Respectueux - Respectueuse Adj | Respectful

— *Le **respect** dans un couple est important* • Respect in a couple
is important

RESPIRER

1. Respirer v | To breathe
2. La respiration nf | The respiration
3. Respiratoire Adj | Respiratory
4. Un respirateur nm | A ventilator

   — *Le patient est sous **respirateur*** • The patient is on a ventilator

RESPONSABLE

1. Responsable Adj | Responsible
2. Une responsabilité nf | A responsibility
3. Responsabiliser v | To empower

— *Boire et conduire n'est pas **responsable*** • Drinking and driving is
not responsible

RESTAURANT

1. Un restaurant nm | A restaurant
2. La restauration nf | The catering

— *Ce nouveau **restaurant** est très bien noté* • This new restaurant
is highly rated

RETRAITE

1. La retraite nf | The retirement
2. Retraiter v | To retire
3. Un retraité nm | A retiree
4. Une retraitée nf | A retiree

— *Mes parents sont à la **retraire** depuis 2 ans* • My parents have
been retired for 2 years

RÉUSSIR

1. Réussir v | To succeed
2. Réussi - Réussie Adj | Achieved
3. Une réussite nf | A success

*Il doit sa **réussite** à son propre travail* • He owes his success to his own work

RÊVE

1. Un rêve nm | A dream
2. Rêver v | To dream

— *Les **rêves** sont parfois réalistes* • Dreams are sometimes realistic

RÉVISER

1. Réviser v | To review
2. Une révision nf | A review
3. Un réviseur nm | A reviser
4. Une réviseuse nf | A reviser
5. Révisable Adj | Revisable

— *Il **révise** ses notes avant la présentation* • He reviews his notes before the presentation

RICHE

1. Riche Adj | Rich
2. La richesse nf | The wealth

— *Être **riche** est le but de beaucoup de personnes* • Being rich is the goal of many people

RIRE

1. Rire v | To laugh
2. Le rire nm | The laugh

— *Le **rire** est communicatif* • Laughing is communicative

RISQUE

1. Un risque nm | A risk
2. Risquer v | To risk

— *Peu de personnes aiment prendre des **risques*** • Not many people like to take risks

ROMANCE

1. Une romance nf | A romance
2. Romantique Adj | Romantic
3. Le romantisme nm | The romantism

— *La demande en mariage était incroyablement* **romantique** •
The proposal was incredibly romantic

ROULER

1. Rouler v | To roll
2. Roulant - Roulante Adj | Rolling
3. Un roulement nm | A roll
4. Un tapis roulant nm | A treadmill

— *Elle passe des heures sur le* **tapis roulant** • She spends hours on
the treadmill

ROYAUME

1. Le royaume nm | The kingdom
2. La royauté nf | The royalty
3. Le roi nm | The king

— *La fête du* **roi** *est toujours en juillet* • The kings' celebration is always in
July

Ss.

SAGE

1. Sage Adj | Wise
2. La sagesse nf | The wisdom
3. Sagement Adv | Wisely
— *Les enfants jouent* **sagement** *dans le jardin* • The children are playing wisely in the yard

SAISON

1. Une saison nf | A season
2. Saisonnier - Saisonnière Adj | Seasonal
— *L'hiver est une* **saison** *froide* • Winter is a cold season

SALADE

1. Une salade nf | A salad
2. Un saladier nm | A salad bowl
3. Une salade de fruits nf | A fruit salad
— *Mon snack préféré est une* **salade** *de fruits* • My favourite snack is a fruit salad

SALE

1. Sale Adj | Dirty
2. Salir v | To dirty
3. La saleté nf | The dirt
— *La salle de bain est* **sale** • The bathroom is dirty

SARCASME

1. Le sarcasme nm | The sarcasm
2. Sarcastique Adj | Sarcastic
— *Ses paroles sont remplies de* **sarcasme** • His words are full of sarcasm

SATISFAIRE

1. Satisfaire v | To satisfy
2. Satisfait - Satisfaite Adj | Satisfied
3. La satisfaction nf | The satisfaction

4. Satisfaisant - Satisfaisante Adj | Satisfactory

— *La **satisfaction** du client est primordiale* • The client's satisfaction is essential

SAUCE

1. Une sauce nf | A sauce
2. Une saucière nf | A saucer

— *Verse la **sauce** dans la **saucière*** • Pour the sauce into the saucer

SAVOIR

1. Savoir v | To know
2. Le savoir nm | The knowledge
3. Un savant nm | A savant
4. Une savante nf | A savant

— *Elle **sait** cuisiner* • She knows how to cook

SAVON

1. Un savon nm | A soap
2. Une savonnette nf | A soap
3. Savonner v | To soap
4. Savonneux - Savonneuse Adj | Soapy
5. Le savon liquide nm | The liquid soap
6. Un distributeur de savon nm | A soap dispenser

— *Elle a offert des **savons** fait maison* • She gifted homemade soaps

SCIENCE

1. Les sciences nf | Science
2. Scientifique Adj | Scientific
3. Un scientifique nm | A scientist
4. Une scientifique nf | A scientist
5. Scientifiquement Adv | Scientifically

— *Le **scientifique** travaille dans un laboratoire* • The scientist works in a laboratory

SCINTILLER

1. Scintiller v | To sparkle
2. Scintillant - Scintillante Adj | Sparkly
3. Un scintillement nm | A sparkle

— *Son collier est **scintillant*** • Her necklace is sparkly

SCULPTER

1. Sculpter v | To sculpt
2. Une sculpture nf | A sculpture
3. Un sculpteur nm | A sculptor
4. Une sculptrice nf | A sculptor

— *La **sculpture** dans son jardin est imposante* • The sculpture in his yard is imposing

SÉCHER

1. Sécher v | To dry
2. Le séchage nm | The drying
3. Sec - Sèche Adj | Dry
4. La sècheresse nf | The drought
5. Le dessèchement nm | The dryness
6. Un sèche-cheveux nm | A hairdryer
7. Un séchoir nm | A dryer

— *Je me **sèche** les cheveux et je suis prête* • I'm drying my hair and then I'll be ready

SECOURS

1. Le secours nm | The aid
2. Secourir v | To rescue
3. Un secouriste nm | A rescuer
4. Une secouriste nf | A rescuer

— *Le **secouriste** fait son possible pour traiter la personne accidentée* • The rescuer does his best to treat the injured person

SECRÉTARIAT

1. Le secrétariat nf | The reception

2. Un secrétaire nm | A secretary

3. Une secrétaire nf | A secretary

— *Le colis vous attend au **secrétariat*** • The package is waiting for you at the reception

SÉCURISER

1. Sécuriser v | To secure

2. La sécurisation nf | The securing

3. La sécurité nf | The safety

4. Un agent de sécurité nm | A security guard

— *L'**agent de sécurité** travaille souvent la nuit* • The security guard often works at night

SÉJOUR

1. Un séjour nm | A stay

2. Séjourner v | To stay

— *Nous **séjournerons** dans cet hôtel* • We will stay at this hotel

SÉLECTION

1. Une sélection nf | A selection

2. Sélectionner v | To select

— *Il a **sélectionné** les matières qu'il veut apprendre* • He selected the fields he wants to learn

SÉNAT

1. Le Sénat nm | The Senate

2. Un sénateur nm | A senator

3. Une sénatrice nf | A senator

— *Elle a été élue **sénatrice** récemment* • She got elected as senator recently

SENTIR

1. Sentir v | To smell

2. Une senteur nf | A scent

— *Cette bougie parfumée **sent** trop fort* • This scented candle smells too strong

SÉPARER

1. Séparer v | To separate
2. La séparation nf | The separation
3. Un séparateur nm | A separator
4. Inséparable Adj | Inseparable

— *Le **séparateur** permet de garder les tiroirs organisés* • The separator keeps the drawers organised

SÉRIEUX

1. Sérieux - Sérieuse Adj | Serious
2. Sérieusement Adv | Seriously

— *Parle-t-il **sérieusement** ?* • Is he speaking seriously?

SERPENT

1. Un serpent nm | A snake
2. Serpenter v | To meander

— *Le **serpent** aime se cacher dans le sable* • The serpent likes to hide in the sand

SERVIR

1. Servir v | To serve
2. Le serveur nm | The server
3. La serveuse nf | The server
4. Le servant nm | The servant
5. La servante nf | The servant
6. Le service nm | The service

— *La **serveuse** va apporter le menu dans une minute* • The waitress will bring the menu in a minute

SEXE

1. Le sexe nm | Sex
2. Le sexe masculin nm | Male

3. Le sexe féminin nm | Female

4. Sexuel - Sexuelle Adj | Sexual

5. La sexualité nf | The sexuality

— *L'éducation **sexuelle** est enseignée à l'école* • Sexual education is taught at school

SIGNIFIER

1. Signifier v | To mean / To signify

2. Une signification nf | A signification

3. Significatif - Significative Adj | Significant

— *La **signification** des écrits anciens est toujours un mystère* • The signification of ancients writing is still a mystery

SIMPLE

1. Simple Adj | Simple

2. Simplement Adv | Simply

3. Simplifier v | To simplify

4. Un aller simple nm | A one-way ticket

— *J'ai réservé un **aller simple** pour la Floride* • I booked a one-way ticket to Florida

SKI

1. Un ski nm | A ski

2. Skier v | To ski

3. Un skieur nm | A skier

4. Une skieuse nf | A skier

— *Il a perdu un **ski** dans sa chute* • He lost a ski in the fall

SOIGNER

1. Soigner v | To nurse

2. Un aide-soignant nm | A caregiver

3. Une aide-soignante nf | A caregiver

4. Soigneux - Soigneuse Adj | Careful

5. Soigneusement Adv | Carefully

6. Un soin nm | A care

— *L'**aide-soignant** vient tous les jours à la maison pour changer son bandage* • The caregiver comes to his home every day to change his bandage

SOIR

1. Le soir nm | The evening
2. La soirée nf | The evening
3. Bonsoir nm | Good evening

— *Les **soirées** d'hiver sont parfois longues* • Winter evenings are sometimes longs

SOLIDE

1. Solide Adj | Solid
2. La solidité nf | The strength / Solidity
3. Solidement Adv | Solidly
4. Solidaire Adj | Solidary

— *Cette cabane est **solide*** • This shed is solid

SOUS

1. Sous Prép | Below
2. Le sous-sol nm | The basement
3. Un sous-plat nm | A potholder
4. Un sous-verre nm | A coaster
5. Un sous-vêtement nm | Underwear

— *La machine à laver se trouve au **sous-sol*** • The washing machine is in the basement

SOUVENIR

1. Souvenir v | To recall
2. Un souvenir nm | A memory

— *Les **souvenirs** sont importants pour la mémoire* • Memories are important for the memory

SPÉCIALISER

1. Spécialiser v | To specialize

2. Un spécialiste nm | A specialist

3. Une spécialiste nf | A specialist

4. Une spécialité nf | A specialty

5. Spécial - Spéciale Adj | Special

— *Il va bientôt choisir sa **spécialité** pour ses études* • He will soon choose his specialty for his studies

SPECTACLE

1. Un spectacle nm | A show

2. Spectaculaire Adj | Spectacular

3. Un spectateur nm | A spectator

4. Une spectatrice nf | A spectator

— *Le nouveau **spectacle** est enfin prêt* • The new show is finally ready

SPORT

1. Le sport nm | The sport

2. Sportif - Sportive Adj | Sportive

3. Le sport d'hiver nm | Winter sport

*Quel **sport** pratique-t-elle ?* • What sport does she practice?

STABILISER

1. Stabiliser v | To stabilise

2. Un stabilisateur nm | A stabiliser

3. La stabilisation nf | The stabilisation

4. La stabilité nf | The stability

5. Stable Adj | Stable

— *Le bateau a des problèmes de **stabilité*** •The boat has some stability problems

STAGE

1. Un stage nm | An internship

2. Un stagiaire nm | An intern

3. Une stagiaire nf | An intern

— *Mon fils a decroché un **stage*** • My son got an internship

SUCRE

1. Le sucre nm | The sugar
2. Sucré - Sucrée Adj | Sweet
3. Un sucrier nm | A sugar bowl
4. Une sucrerie nf | A sugar refinery
5. Sucrer v | To sweeten

— *Le **sucre** est mauvais pour les dents* • Sugar is bad for your teeth

SUGGÉRER

1. Suggérer v | To suggest
2. Une suggestion nf | A suggestion

— *Puis-je **suggérer** une idée ?* • Can I suggest an idea?

SUPPORTER

1. Supporter v | To support
2. Le support nm | The support
3. Un supporteur nm | A supporter
4. Une supportrice nf | A supporter

— *Le parti politique a beaucoup de **support*** • The political party has a lot of support

SÛR

1. Sûr Adj | Sure
2. Sûrement Adv | Surely
3. La sûreté nf | The safety

— *Mon père connaît **sûrement** la réponse* • My father surely knows the answer

SURPRENDRE

1. Surprendre v | To surprise
2. Surpris - Surprise Adj | Surprised
3. La surprise nf | The surprise
4. Surprenant - Surprenante Adj | Surprising

— *Elle ne sait pas qu'elle va recevoir une **surprise*** • She doesn't know that she will get a surprise

T t.

TAILLER

1. Tailler v | To size
2. Une taille nf | A size
3. Un tailleur nm | A tailor
4. Un tailleur nm | A suit

—— *Est-ce que je peux essayer ce pantalon une **taille** au-dessus ?* • Can I try these pants a size bigger?

TALENT

1. Un talent nm | A talent
2. Talentueux - Talentueuse Adj | Talented

—— *Cette chanteuse a un immense **talent*** • This singer has immense talent

TAPIS

1. Un tapis nm | A carpet
2. Une tapisserie nf | A tapestry
Tapisser v | To line

—— *Le **tapis** sera livré lundi* • The carpet will be delivered on Monday

TAXE

1. Une taxe nf | A tax
2. Taxer v | To tax
3. Une taxation nf | A taxation

—— *Les **taxes** augmenteront de 5% en 2021* • Taxes will increase by 5% in 2021

TECHNIQUE

1. La technique nf | A technique
2. Technique Adj | Technical
3. Un technicien nm | A technician
4. Une technicienne nf | A technician
5. La technologie nf | Technology

—— *Le **technicien** tente de réparer la panne* • The technician tries to fix the breakdown

TÉLÉPHONE

1. Un téléphone nm | A phone
2. Téléphoner v | To call
3. Un appel téléphonique nm | A phone call

— *Je lui **téléphone** dans une minute* • I will call her in a minute

TÉMOIN

1. Un témoin nm | A witness
2. Témoigner v | To witness
3. Un témoignage nm | A testimony

— *Son **témoignage** est la clé de cette enquête* • His testimony is the key of this investigation

TEMPÉRER

1. Tempérer v | To temper
2. La température nf | The temperature

— *La **température** du corps est 37 degrés* • Body temperature is 37 degrees

TÊTE

1. La tête nf | The head
2. Un mal de tête nm | A headache
3. Têtu - Têtue Adj | Stubborn

— *Ce petit garçon est **têtu*** • This little boy is stubborn

TOIT

1. Un toit nm | A roof
2. La toiture nf | A roof

— *Il y a une fuite dans la **toiture*** • There is a leak in the roof

TÔT

1. Tôt Adv | Early
2. Aussitôt Adv | Instantly

— *Tu te lèves **tôt** aujourd'hui* • You are getting up early today

176

TOTAL

1. Le total nm | The total
2. Totaliser v | To total
3. Totalement Adv | Totally
   — *Le **total** de la facture est de 320$* • The total of the bill is $320

TOUSSER

1. Tousser v | To cough
2. Une toux nf | A cough
   — *Il **tousse** depuis hier, il va rester à la maison* • He has been coughing since yesterday, he will stay at home

TRADITION

1. Une tradition nf | A tradition
2. Traditionnel - Traditionnelle Adj | Traditional
   — *Le repas de ce soir est **traditionnel*** • The meal tonight is traditional

TRADUIRE

1. Traduire v | To translate
2. Une traduction nf | A translation
3. Un traducteur nm | A translator
4. Une traductrice nf | A translator
   — *La **traduction** de ce document ne semble pas correcte* • The translation of this document doesn't seem accurate

TRAÎNER

1. Traîner v | To drag
2. Un traîneau nm | A sled
3. Un chien de traîneau nm | A sled dog
   — *Les **chiens de traîneau** sont souvent des Huskies* • Sled dogs are often Huskies

TRAITER

1. Traiter v | To treat

2. Un traitement nm | A treatment

— *Le **traitement** doit être pris tous les jours* • The treatment has to be taken everyday

TRANSFORMER

1. Transformer v | To transform

2. Une transformation nf | A transformation

— *Les panneaux solaires **transforment** les rayons du soleil en énergie* • Solar panels transform sunlight into energy

TRANSPORT

1. Le transport nm | The transport

2. Transporter v | To transport

3. Transportable Adj | Transportable

4. Un transporteur nm | A transporter

5. Une transportation nf | A transportation

6. Le transport en commun nm | Public transit

— *Le **transport en commun** est en grève* • Public transit is on strike

TRAVAIL

1. Le travail nm | The work

2. Travailler v | To work

3. Un travailleur nm | A worker

4. Une travailleuse nf | A worker

— *Je marche pour aller au **travail** le matin* • I walk to work in the morning

TRAVERSER

1. Traverser v | To cross

2. À travers Prép | Across

— *La famille **traverse** la route au feu rouge* • The family crosses the road at the red light

TRISTE

1. Triste Adj | Sad

2. Tristement Adv | Sadly

3. La tristesse nf | The sadness

— *Le film que j'ai regardé hier m'a rendu **triste*** • The movie I watched yesterday made me feel sad

TROU

1. Un trou nm | A hole

2. Trouer v | To hole

— *Le jardinier creuse un **trou** pour planter un arbre* • The landscaper digs a hole to plant a tree

TROUVER

1. Trouver v | To find

2. Trouvable Adj | Trackable

3. Introuvable Adj | Untraceable

4. Une trouvaille nf | A find

— *Son téléphone reste **introuvable*** • His phone is still untraceable

TUER

1. Tuer v | To kill

2. Un tueur nm | A killer

3. Un tueur en série nm | A serial killer

— *Le **tueur en série** a été condamné à la prison à vie* • The serial killer was sentenced to life in prison

Uu.

UNIFORME

1. Un uniforme nm | A uniform
2. Uniformiser v | To standardize
3. Une uniformité nf | The uniformity

— *Dans une école privée, vous devez porter un **uniforme*** • In a private school, you have to wear a uniform

UNIR

1. Unir v | To unite
2. Uni - Unie Adj | United
3. Une union nf | A union

— *Le mariage est une **union*** • Marriage is a union

UNIVERS

1. L'univers nm | The universe
2. Universel - Universelle Adj | Universal

— *La Terre est une planète dans l'**univers*** • Earth is a planet in the universe

UNIVERSITÉ

1. Une université nf | A university
2. Universitaire Adj | Academic

— *L'Anglettere est connue pour ses **universités** prestigieuses* • England is known for its prestigious universities

USER

1. User v | To use
2. L'usage nm | The use

— *La garantie couvre seulement un **usage** normal du produit* • The warranty only covers normal use of the product

UTILE

1. Utile Adj | Useful
2. L'utilité nf | The utility
3. Utiliser v | To use

— ***Utilise** de l'eau de javel pour nettoyer* • Use bleach to clean

Vv.

VACANCES

1. Les vacances nf | The vacation
2. Un vacancier nm | A vacationer
3. Une vacancière nf | A vacationer
4. Bonnes vacances | Happy holidays

— *J'ai tellement besoin de **vacances*** • I really need a vacation

VALIDER

1. Valider v | To validate
2. Une validation nf | A validation
3. La validité nf | The validity
4. Valide Adj | Valid

— *Je dois **valider** mon ticket de parking* • I need to validate my parking ticket

VÉHICULE

1. Un véhicule nm | A vehicle
2. Véhiculer v | To convey

— *Mon **véhicule** a besoin de réparations* • My vehicle needs repairs

VENTE

1. La vente nf | The sale
2. Vendre v | To sell
3. Un vendeur nm | A salesperson
4. Une vendeuse nf | A salesperson

— *La maison d'en face est à **vendre*** • The house across is for sale

VENTILER

1. Ventiler v | To ventilate
2. Un ventilateur nm | A fan
3. La ventilation nf | The ventilation

— *Un **ventilateur** est une nécessité pendant l'été* • A fan is a necessity during summer

VENTRE

1. Le ventre nm | The stomach
2. Un ventriloque nm | A ventriloquist
3. Un mal de ventre nm | A stomachache

— *J'ai vu ce **ventriloque** il y a quelques années* • I saw this ventriloquist few years ago

VÉRIFIER

1. Vérifier v | To verify
2. Une vérification nf | A verification
3. Un vérificateur nm | An inspector
4. Une vérificatrice nf | An inspector
5. Vérifiable Adj | Verifiable

— *La police **vérifie** l'identité des passagers* • The police verify the identity of the passengers

VERNIR

1. Vernir v | To varnish
2. Un vernis nm | A varnish
3. Un vernis à ongles nm | A nail polish
4. Le vernissage nm | The coating

— *La table de la salle à manger vient d'être **vernie*** • The table in the living room just got varnished

VERSER

1. Verser v | To pour
2. Un versement nm | A payment

— *Le **versement** est arrivé ce matin sur le compte* • The payment arrived this morning in the account

VICTOIRE

1. Une victoire nf | A victory
2. Victorieux - Victorieuse Adj | Victorious

— *L'équipe des filles a remporté la **victoire*** • The girls team won the victory

VIGNE

1. Une vigne nf | A vine
2. Un vignoble nm | A vineyard
3. Un vigneron nm | A winemaker
4. Une vigneronne nf | A winemaker
5. Le vin nm | The wine

— *Il y a de magnifiques **vignobles** en Colombie-Britannique* • There are beautiful vineyards in British Columbia

VILLAGE

1. Un village nm | A village
2. Un villageois nm | A villager
3. Une villageoise nf | A villager

— *Durant la guerre, beaucoup de **villages** ont été détruits* • During the war, a lot of villages were ruined

VIOL

1. Un viol nm | A rape
2. Violer v | To rape
3. Une violation nf | A violation
4. La violence nf | The violence
5. Violent - Violente Adj | Violent

— *Il est accusé de **viol** par sa collègue* • He is accused of rape by his colleague

VIRER

1. Virer v | To transfer
2. Un virement nm | A transfer

— *L'argent a été **viré** la semaine dernière* • The money was transferred last week

VIRTUEL

1. Virtuel - Virtuelle Adj | Virtual
2. La virtualité nf | The virtuality

—— *Les jeux **virtuels** sont de plus en plus populaires* • Virtual games are more and more popular

VISION

1. Une vision nf | A vision
2. Visionner v | To watch / To view
3. Un visionnaire nm | A visionary
4. Une visionnaire nf | A visionary
5. Visible Adj | Visible
6. La visibilité nf | The visibility

—— *Les cyclistes portent des vêtements clairs pour la **visibilité*** • Bikers wear light colored clothes for visibility

VISITE

1. Une visite nf | A visit
2. Visiter v | To visit
3. Un visiteur nm | A visitor
4. Une visite guidée nf | A guided tour
5. Une carte de visite nf | A business card

—— *La **visite guidée** du musée était passionnante* • The guided tour of the museum was exciting

VIVRE

1. Vivre v | To live
2. Vivant - Vivante Adj | Alive
3. La vie nf | The life
4. Vital - Vitale Adj | Vital

—— *Une transplantation de cœur est **vitale** pour lui* • A heart transplant is vital for him

VOISIN

1. Un voisin nm | A neighbor
2. Une voisine nf | A neighbor
3. Le voisinage nm | The neighbourhood

— Les nouveaux **voisins** organisent un diner pour rencontrer le voisinage • The new neighbors are organizing a dinner to meet the neighbourhood

VOITURE

1. Une voiture nf | A car
2. Un voiturier nm | A valet

— Les nouvelles **voitures** sont de plus en plus écologiques • New cars are more and more environmentally friendly

VOLCAN

1. Un volcan nm | A volcano
2. Volcanique Adj | Volcanic

— Les **volcans** d'Hawaii offrent un paysage indescriptible • Volcanoes in Hawaii offer an indescribable landscape

VOULOIR

1. Vouloir v | To want
2. Voulu - Voulue Adj | Wanting

— Les jumeaux **veulent** de nouveaux vélos pour leurs anniversaires • The twins want new bikes for their birthdays

VOYAGE

1. Un voyage nm | A travel
2. Voyager v | To travel
3. Un voyageur nm | A voyager
4. Une voyageuse nf | A voyager
5. Une agence de voyage nf | A travel agency

— Cette **agence de voyage** propose des vacances à prix abordables • This travel agency has vacations for an affordable price

Ww.

WEB

1. Le web nm | The web
2. Un site web nm | A website
3. Une webcam nf | A webcam
4. Un webinaire nm | A webinar

— *Les **sites web** permettent aux entreprises d'être plus visibles •*
Websites allow companies to be more visible

Yy.

YAOURT

1. Un yaourt nm | A yogurt

2. Une yaourtière nf | A yogurt maker

— *Elle fait tous ses **yaourts** maisons* • She makes all her yogurts at home

YOGA

1. Le yoga nm | Yoga

2. Un yogi nm | A yogi

3. Une yogi nf | A yogi

— *Cette séance de **yoga** était particulièrement relaxante* • This yoga session was particularly relaxing

ANNEXE

A

193

B

194

C

196

D

198

E

F

G

H

I

204

M

$\mathcal{N}$

208

Q

R

S

212

T

214

Made in the USA
Las Vegas, NV
12 January 2024